STILL CATHOLIC

After All These Years

Also by the authors of
STILL CATHOLIC AFTER ALL THESE YEARS:

Growing Up Catholic
More Growing Up Catholic

Still
CATHOLIC
After All These Years

MARY JANE FRANCES CAVOLINA MEARA

JEFFREY ALLEN JOSEPH STONE

MAUREEN ANNE TERESA KELLY

RICHARD GLEN MICHAEL DAVIS

ILLUSTRATIONS BY BOB JONES

A MAIN STREET BOOK

NEW YORK LONDON TORONTO SYDNEY AUCKLAND

A MAIN STREET BOOK
PUBLISHED BY DOUBLEDAY
a division of Bantam Doubleday Dell Publishing Group, Inc.
1540 Broadway, New York, New York 10036

MAIN STREET BOOKS, DOUBLEDAY, and the portrayal of a building with a
tree are trademarks of Doubleday, a division of Bantam Doubleday
Dell Publishing Group, Inc.

Photography Credits:
Sister Catherine Grabowski, R.S.M.: pages 7, 11, 31, 39, 40, 50, 53, 60, 61, 62, 63, 101
Alinari/Art Resource, N.Y.: pages 43, 44, 45 (bottom)
Scala/Art Resource, N.Y.: page 45 (top)
Marburg/Art Resource, N.Y.: page 46 (top and bottom)
Art Resource, N.Y.: page 47
AP/Wide World Photos: pages 58, 73 (top and bottom), 74, 76 (top and bottom), 77, 86,
98 (top), 100, 104
Giraudon/Art Resource, N.Y.: page 72
The Bettmann Archive: pages 84, 89, 90

Library of Congress Cataloging-in-Publication Data
Still Catholic after all these years / Mary Jane Frances Cavolina
    Meara : illustrations by Bob Jones. – 1st ed.
        p.   cm.
    1. Catholic Church–United States–History–20th century–Humor.
    2. Catholic wit and humor. 3. American wit and humor. 4. United
    States–Church history–20th century–Humor. I. Meara, Mary Jane
    Frances Cavolina, 1954–
    BX1406.2.S745 1993
    282'.73'0207–dc20   93-9935
                                                                     CIP

ISBN 0-385-42546-5

1 3 5 7 9 10 8 6 4 2

ACKNOWLEDGMENTS

We have drawn heavily on the anecdotes, expertise, and indulgence of our friends, colleagues, and families in the writing of this book. It is not enough to say that their perspectives and contributions have enriched it immensely; without their help, writing it would have been simply impossible. We would like to thank the following people in particular:

David Gernert, for his immediate grasp of and enthusiasm for our idea; Bruce Tracy, for his intelligence, attention to detail, sure sense of comic timing, and sensitivity to our material; and Richard Pine, for his friendship, early support, and diligent efforts on our behalf—not bad for a bunch of non-Catholics.

The following friends must be thanked especially for their extraordinary and invaluable help: Mary Meara Braunstein; Jared Brenner; Jim Davis; Michele Farinet; Sister Catherine Grabowski, R.S.M., for the original photographs, and her models—Sister Mary Estelle Conaty, R.S.M., and Sister Betty Calfapietra, R.S.M.; and Robert LeVulis.

For their never-failing friendship, encouragement, good humor, and assistance: F. Amoy Allen, Shaye Areheart, Deborah Berardi, Rho Burke, Msgr. John T. Casey, Valery DeCola, John Dempsey, Lisa Dunning, John Dynes, Sister Joan Ersing, Roy Finamore, Larry Friend, Father Francis Gasparik, O.F.M. Cap., Peter St. John Ginna, David Groff, Janet Jaffke, Maxx Kanzler, Liddy Kelly, Michael LaFleur, Jim Landis, Ileana Lara, Michael Lee, M.D., Raymond Lefebvre, Karen and Joe Lizzi, Paul Mahon, Erica Marcus, Dick Marek, Janice Meagher, Michelle, Mindi Miller, Mike and Mary Monks, Nadia Pappas, Jeff Phillips, Carol and Craig Pineau, Betty Prashker, Joseph Raimondi, Dot Romanov Regina, Meg Ruley, Michelle Sidrane, Cheryl Smart-Zukof, Sharon Squibb, Kathleen Starger, Steve Topping, Lorrie Tosiello, Jim Wade, Morty and Sylvia Witt, Henny Youngman; and the folks at: Barber's Bookstore, Bill's Unocal 76, Leo's

Lunch Room, Midwest Roofing Specialists (Rick, Tony, Kelly, Batman, Fruitfly, and Fishhead), and West Crystal Street.

And for their enthusiasm and love, our families, who helped us grow up Catholic, become more Catholic, and stay Catholic: the Flying Cavolinas—Robbie, Lisa, Ellen and Josh, Larry and Lorraine, Michael and Joan; Brian Meara; Charlie and Ethel Meara; Anne and Norman Stone; Greg and Ted Stone; Liz and Larry Strach; Sue and Phil Slocum; the Flaherty family; Anne and Mike Keehnen, and Liam and Collette; Kevin Kelly and Claire Cappelle; Patrick and Vincent Kelly; Don and Eileen Davis; Sharon Carroll; Chris and Sue Kourim; Jackie Kourim; Peter Kourim; Tom and Therese Kourim.

WITH LOVE TO
FRANK AND SHIRLEY CAVOLINA;
MICHELLE, AMY, JAKE, ANDREW, DANIELLE, AND CAMERON;
JIM AND ETHAN BUSIS;
DONALD AND RITA DAVIS, AND DON AND SHAWN DIEBOLD

CONTENTS

STILL CATHOLIC

After All These Years

INTRODUCTION

✝

In our books *Growing Up Catholic* and *More Growing Up Catholic,* we looked back on the Roman Catholic Church of our childhood—the Church of ruler-wielding nuns, of fish on Fridays, and of getting two Our Fathers and three Hail Marys for your penance no matter how bad your sins were. But the trappings of that old, pre-Vatican II Church have now vanished almost entirely, except in the bittersweet memories of millions of thirty-something-and-above Catholics.

A whole new generation of Catholics has grown up without ever hearing a word of Latin at Mass, or seeing a wimple except in a movie or on Halloween. Meanwhile, many older Catholics find the new Church almost unrecognizable, and are left with a sense of loss so great they may feel compelled to call upon St. Anthony for help. ("St. Anthony, St. Anthony, please come around. Something is lost and cannot be found.")

Instead of the old certainties of the past, today's Church offers change and choice. Some of the choices may seem minor—like whether to take Communion in your hand or on your tongue, or whether to receive the Sacrament of Reconciliation (formerly known as Confession) anonymously or sitting face to face with a priest. But to Catholics raised to believe that there was only one way to do a host of things, the very idea of choice is revolutionary.

Small wonder, then, that Catholics now challenge Church stances that the Vatican considers closed subjects. Pope John Paul II may rail against what he calls "cafeteria Catholics"—Catholics who pick and choose among the Church's official teachings—but when the Church started to change, a questioning spirit was awakened.

Has the Catholic Church changed too little or too much? You'll hear both points of view, although judging from recent polls, more American Catholics would say "too little" than "too much." One thing is certain: the debate will continue ad infinitum (and perhaps ad nauseam) as the institution tries to strike a balance between tradition and modern needs.

So how do we tell if we're still Catholic? The Catholicism of the past relied heavily on the outward signs of faith—on following Church regulations and on observing a rigid, prescribed code of behavior. If you played by the rules, you were a Good Catholic and you went to Heaven, perhaps with a pit stop in Purgatory. Of course, following the rules alone did not make you a Good Catholic. Recognizing this, today's Catholics tend to look inward to find the anchor of their spirituality, but sometimes forget the support that ritual and community can provide.

Yet despite appearances, the core of our Catholicism is fundamentally unchanged. Modern and traditional Catholics alike believe that each human being is ultimately responsible for his or her actions, and that those actions have real, even eternal, consequences. The old Church favored the term "examination of conscience." Modern Catholics might not use those words exactly, but they share with traditionalists a basic Catholic reflex, forever asking: Was what I did right or wrong? Good or evil? How can I do better next time?

In *Still Catholic After All These Years,* we take a look at what it's like to be a Catholic today, when all the rules have changed. By the way, you are still Catholic, aren't you? And please don't give us that ex-Catholic routine. There's no such thing and you know it.

I

AM I STILL A CATHOLIC?

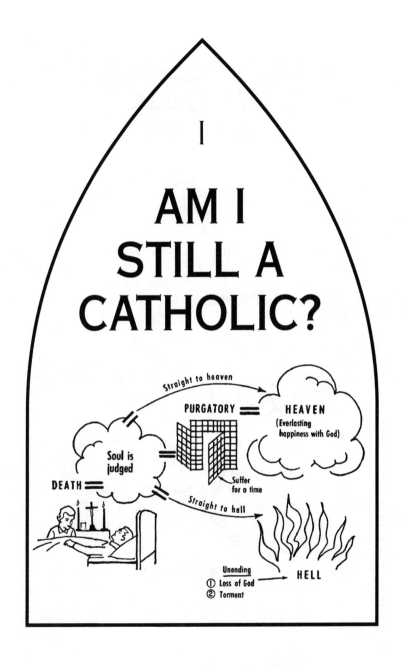

ARE YOU STILL CATHOLIC?:
The Quiz

1. Do you still get a spiritual buzz when they burn incense on holy days?
2. Do you go out of your way to greet priests and nuns you don't know when you meet them on the street? ("Afternoon, Father . . .")
3. Do you find yourself speaking Latin at cocktail parties to impress your friends?
4. Do you do this even when the cocktail party is full of non-Catholics?
5. Do you love to tell people what it was like to go to Confession in the old days?
6. Do you carry a rosary, old holy cards, or a frayed scapular on your person?
7. Have you taken to going to church in ethnic neighborhoods so that you can relive the days when Mass was in Latin?
8. Does every self-help or meditation book you read remind you vaguely of something you learned in Catholic school?
9. Do you find yourself thinking it might not be so bad to have another Italian Pope?
10. Does lighting a candle in church seem strangely comforting?

Score two points for each yes answer:

0–4 pts.	No, you are not.
6–8 pts.	Hated going to parochial school but loved going to church.
10–12 pts.	Lapsed, but longing for that old-time religion.
14–16 pts.	Devout churchgoer.
18–20 pts.	Quit fooling around. You are a priest or a nun.

ONE FROM COLUMN A:
Cafeteria Catholics

In the old days, being Catholic was akin to taking the "set menu" at the Cafeteria of Catholicism. The devoted were handed a full plate, steaming with doctrines, traditions, and unwritten rules to live by. Sure, there were the optional side dishes, but by and large, the same dishes on the menu in Rome became the standard meal at Cafeterias all over the world.

Some Catholics' tastes may have become a little more gourmet these days because the same old chow doesn't look as appetizing to them as it once did. These Catholics who don't automatically reach for the blue plate special are known as

Cafeteria Catholics, a phrase used pejoratively by Pope John Paul II. They stroll down the line picking and choosing what looks good to them, often with much discussion about the pros and cons of each offering, and leave the rest behind.

Take Craig and Carol Porter, your average Cafeteria Catholics, who stopped by the Cafeteria for dinner the other evening. They both passed on the appetizer special that day, the unpopular Rhythm Method of Birth Control. Instead, Craig picked up a serving of can't-go-wrong Ten Commandments, and Carol chose Parochial School for Children, which looked especially substantial and tasty.

On to the main course. Carol had heard that the Cafeteria might begin to offer Female Priests, but the manager said that despite the many requests, they hadn't gotten the recipe right and that dish would have to wait. She was tempted by the Holy Days of Obligation, and the Daily Mass looked pretty good, but decided on Lenten Observances with a side order of Easter Vigil. Craig inspected the Celibate Priests, which looked a little stale, and selected Devotion to Patron Saints, which he always enjoyed.

The array of tempting desserts looked delicious, especially the Miraculous Medal Devotion, Votive Candles, Family Prayer, and Ash Wednesday. After much debate, Craig opted for a bowl of Advent Calendars and Carol was delighted that the St. Blaise Day Blessing of Throats was available. Satisfied with the dishes they had selected, Craig and Carol left the Cafeteria looking forward to their next visit.

AS IT WAS IN THE BEGINNING:
The Old Guard

Within the brave new post–Vatican II world there exists a secret cell, a gentle cabal if you will, of the meekest subversives the Church has ever seen. It is made up of men and women in their fifties, sixties, and seventies who, no matter how infirm, would never even think of crossing the center aisle of the church without a proper genuflection, no matter how casual the rest of the congregation has become. They will not take the Host from the lay server in their hands. They don't much care for the notion of lay servers anyway. They wait for their beloved Church to come to its senses and put things back the way they were. In the meantime, they discreetly go their own way.

When Father says, "The Lord be with you," observe carefully. Notice that after everyone else says, "And also with you," they are still moving their lips like the actors in a badly dubbed Japanese movie. Did you hear "*etcumspiritutuo*" too? And isn't that a worn missal with yellowed tape on the binding, hidden like a school kid's comic book inside the disposable missalette with the Cubist church on the cover? What *is* that funny writing in that dog-eared little book? Could that be . . . Latin?! Is that a copy of a 1963 *Extension* magazine discreetly tucked in the Sunday paper?

And what about these charming refuseniks' behavior after receiving Communion? They don't—like their post–Vatican II brethren—return to their seats, have a quick chat with God, and immediately sit back in the pew and look around the church as if it were intermission at the theater. No, they kneel down, bury their faces in their hands, and remain on the kneeler until Mass is in full swing again. And they keep kneeling even if they've had knee and hip replacement surgery.

Vatican I is where these recalcitrants grew up, cemented their faith, buried their loved ones, and found their God. And through a smile, they will tell you that they have absolutely no complaint with the post–Vatican II Church, as they dip their hands into the holy water font, genuflect, carefully make the sign of the cross, and recall another era of Catholicism.

THE UNSPOKEN COMMANDMENTS

I. Thou shalt not wear thy Ash Wednesday ashes for more than one day, lest thou want to be taken for an unwashed person.

II. Thou shalt not go out of thy way to pass a church just to make thesign of the cross.

III. Thou shalt not use excessive tithing, like excessive tipping, to show thyself to be a big shot.

IV. Thou shalt not make up outrageous sins to say in the confsional just so thou can get that "squeaky clean" feeling every week.

V. Thou shalt not go back for one more Host at Communion.

VI. Thou shalt not spend so much time in church that thou is mistaken for a homeless person.

VII. Thou shalt not yell "Bingo!" when thou dost not have bingo.

THE PRODIGAL CHILD:
When a Lapsed Catholic Returns to Mass

Major changes in the Mass have been occurring for the past thirty years, and to those who have attended regularly, they no longer come as a great surprise. But many Catholics stopped attending Mass religiously, so to speak, a long time ago. Electric votive candles and women on the altar are only a few of the shocks in store for them should they decide to return.

In place of luxurious clerical garments are more modest vestments—the priestly version of at-home clothes, the sort of thing you'd find in an L. L. Bean catalogue if they made liturgical attire. The priests are not dressing up the way they used to when you come to visit, but neither do your very best friends when you go to their place. And Mass-goers, who used to wear their best garments to God's house, just don't anymore, the way no one seems to doll up to go out to dinner or to a Broadway show these days. Mass-going attire is now decidedly relaxed, casual, and comfortable.

The lapsed Catholic may notice too—like anyone returning home after a long absence—that the furniture has been moved. Not only has the altar been turned around, but in some churches, it's been moved down the sanctuary steps and into the center aisle. The baptismal font is now in a prominent place inside the church, the baptistry has been turned into a Reconciliation Room, and the confessionals have disappeared altogether.

As he ponders the experience of going to a contemporary Mass, the prodigal child may find himself feeling both that something has been lost and that something has been gained. Gone is the awe and mystery of the Latin liturgy, the still and solemn grandeur of the Holy Sacrifice of the Mass. Indeed, the streamlined, contemporary look and feel of today's leaner Mass may at first make the prodigal child feel like a stranger. On the other hand, while

the whole shebang may be less majestic, it's also friendlier and more welcoming.

In place of silent devotion, there's relative chaos—people are singing, people are kissing, people are parading around the church carrying things. Compared to the service of old, it's a virtual orgy of activity. The returnee will find that he can't just attend Mass anymore; he gets dragged into it—less reluctantly, one hopes, than he was dragged into the hokey-pokey at his cousin Mary Camilla's wedding.

SOME THINGS NEVER CHANGE:

What Children Do During a Boring Sermon

Feel yourself dozing off in spite of Father's booming voice? Take comfort in knowing that you're part of a long tradition of Catholics who have trouble concentrating on a homily. Take a tip from the kids, who have always found ways to amuse themselves during the sermon.

1. Play with Gameboy.
2. Count all the lights you can see without moving your head.
3. Guess the time, then turn around to look at the clock and see if you're right.
4. Pull on that loose yarn in your sweater.
5. Eat dry Cheerios.
6. Say the alphabet to yourself backward.
7. Chew gum until taste is gone. Stick under pew.
8. Inspect the row of shoulders in front of you for dandruff.
9. Read the captions on the stained-glass windows. Memorize them.
10. See how long you can hold your breath.

ROMAN CATHOLICS ANONYMOUS:
Catholics and the Recovery Syndrome

Programs like Alcoholics Anonymous, Overeaters Anonymous, and Sexaholics Anonymous have helped millions of people with real problems. The recovery syndrome has swept the nation, and Catholics are not immune to its appeal. In fact, there is now a program, Roman Catholics Anonymous, designed specifically for people who are trying to "get over" being Catholic. Catholics join this program for five reasons: guilt, fear, shame, shame, and more shame.

At their meetings, Recovering Catholics let loose with the truth about the traumas that have fouled up their lives. One R.C. is convinced that his punishment for putting the plastic poo-poo on Sister Renunciata's chair condemned him to life as an orderly in a nursing home. Another R.C. confesses that he used to drop his pencil so he could try to look up Sister Inviolata's habit. He is so ashamed of his behavior that he can no longer have sex.

These and other injustices have led the Catholics in RCA to feel that they must reject their faith entirely. Nevertheless, we suspect that most of them will want a priest when it comes time to meet their Higher Power.

THINGS CATHOLICS ARE AFRAID OF

1. Sex
2. Small dark rooms
3. The color black
4. Authority
5. Standing up to authority
6. Lining up
7. Hell
8. Being too lenient with their children
9. Doing anything wrong

THINGS CATHOLICS ARE GUILTY ABOUT

1. Sex
2. Cheating at solitaire
3. Telling white lies
4. Using the office copy machine for personal business
5. Buying Campbell's soup with a Lipton's coupon
6. Parking at a broken meter
7. Jaywalking
8. Being too strict with their children
9. Refusing to answer the door for the Jehovah's Witnesses

THINGS CATHOLICS ARE ASHAMED OF

1. Sex
2. Their bodies
3. Other people's bodies
4. Watching *9½ Weeks* at home alone
5. Wanting to get rich
6. Getting rich
7. Their thoughts
8. Their words
9. Their deeds

SPLISH SPLASH:
Baptism Revisited

In years past, Catholic parents rushed to baptize their children the moment they were old enough to brave the outdoors and get to the church—usually at six weeks. Today the attitude is more relaxed. Baptisms are generally held—en masse—once a month, but if you've planned a barbecue for the scheduled Saturday, or your older child has a Little League game, it's no big deal to put the holy occasion off another month.

Why the lack of urgency? Perhaps it's because Limbo has closed its doors and can no longer claim the soul of an unbaptized baby. Whatever the reason, attitudes have gotten altogether too devil-may-care.

Baptisms used to be held in the intimate little nook of the church called the baptistry, with its elegant baptismal font, candlelight, stained-glass windows, and marble floor—in fact, all the ambience of a medieval castle. The ceremony was small and so private that even the baby's mother was not invited—only the father and the godparents attended, although sometimes a sibling, aunt, or grandparent tagged along. It was a solemn occasion: the deadly stain of Original Sin was being cleansed away, thus saving the caterwauling infant's immortal soul and admitting him or her into the Holy Catholic Church.

Today baptisms are held in the church proper. Gone is the cozy, hushed atmosphere of the past. The lights are up, the organ is playing, the spirit is festive. The emphasis now is on community. At some baptisms it seems like the whole community is in the church with you—indeed, at baptisms that take place during Sunday Mass, the whole community *is* in the church with you.

In the old days a few drops of water on the forehead represented the ritual washing of the soul. The gentle symbolism was clearly understood by one and all. Now, with nothing left to the imagination, infants are doused with a ladleful of holy water over fonts that look like bathtubs rather than the birdbaths of old. In this, as in so many other things, the Catholic Church, bastion of arcane symbolism, has gone literal.

For those who find about a pint of water pouring down a child's neck too subtle, there remains the option of taking off all the child's clothes in a drafty church (some things never change) and dunking him or her into the baptismal tub not once but three times. And despite all this emphasis on washing, you may listen in vain for the words "Original Sin," the thing they're washing away. It's just not V.C. (Vatican Correct) anymore.

But perhaps the most conspicuously different thing about modern baptism is the purely ceremonial role of the godparents, who were once the leading man and lady of the drama. When the godparents answer the priest's questions on behalf of their godchild, so does everyone else in the church. They often do not even get to hold the baby, once a coveted perk of the job.

Although the godparents still have a big responsibility for the child's spiritual welfare and religious education, they are now supporting players with largely nonspeaking roles in the baptism ritual. There is only one advantage: Father will never find out whether they still remember all the words to the Creed, the Our Father, and the Hail Mary.

IS FINGAR A SAINT'S NAME?:

Baby Naming in the '90s

A saint's name undoubtedly remains the preeminent choice when selecting a name for your Catholic offspring. Classic, always in style. But these days, scores of nonsaint (i.e., heathen) names have climbed in popularity among Catholics and non-Catholics alike.

Brad and *Jennifer* were bad enough, but now "unique" names have become fashionable. Many of these are androgynous, like *Ashton*, *Cassidy*, *Jordan*, *Morgan*, *Taylor*, *Tyler*, and *Whitney*. While some modern parents like the sound of these up-to-date names, traditionalists complain that they aren't really first names at all, but actually WASPy-sounding surnames.

There's been a wave of environmental names like *River* and *Rainbow*, and a sprinkling of place names like *Dakota* and *Denver*. There's also been a quiet trend toward biblical names, especially those from the Old Testament. Witness *Jared*, *Joshua*, *Rachel*, *Rebecca*, *Sarah*, and *Zachary*. But classic saints' names are holding their own, with the continued popularity of names like *Andrew*, *Catherine*, *Christopher*, *Elizabeth*, *Matthew*, and *Michael*.

Catholic parents searching for a distinctive name might consider combining the "unique" and classic trends by selecting a little-known saint's name from the following list. But beware—your child may never forgive you.

Juthwara	Irenaeus
Walburga	Rumwold
Guthiac	Modwenna
Osburga	Enoder
Ethelwin	Polycarp
Gobnet	Bobo
Wulfhilda	Tewdric
Sexburga	Clydog
Botulf	Botvid

The less adventurous might choose from the following list of names that you would have sworn weren't saints' names but are.

Adelaide	Aaron
Rupert	Natalie
Priscilla	Dorothy
Guy	Ralph
Quentin	Emma
Martina	Hilary
Isidora	Maximilian
Colette	Hedda
Marina	Susanna

YOU'VE GOT A FRIEND:

The Sacrament of Reconciliation

Perhaps no sacrament better illustrates the differences between the Church of old and the Church of today than the Sacrament of Reconciliation. It is now possible to sit through a First Reconciliation ceremony and never hear the word *sin*.

Children once lived in mortal terror of staining the pure white milk bottle that was their soul. They were frightened to think that they could offend God so deeply that their spirit would be consigned to the fiery depths of Hell should they die before going to Confession or making a perfect Act of Contrition. This caused them to go to Confession to rinse the bottle clean with some frequency—usually on a weekly basis—and in a state of near panic.

They were forgiven, but they also got penance, a punishment that usually came in the form of prayers. Still, it was worth it: it was not good to have God angry at you. Today, the Sacrament of Reconciliation is more about patching things up than about punishment.

When children experience their First Reconciliation nowadays, their whole family is in attendance. While the little ones go off one by one to the Reconciliation Room, their parents and siblings wait supportively in the pews. The kids don't so much confess their sins as have a friendly chat with Father about "wrong choices"—things they might have done to offend their friends, their family, or themselves, things that, by extension, also offend God. There's no "Bless me, Father"; there's no prepared list of transgressions to recite. When it's over, instead of saying a penance consisting of a couple of Our Fathers and Hail Marys, the children are given "projects" to show that they are truly sorry for what they have done and to help make everyone one big happy family

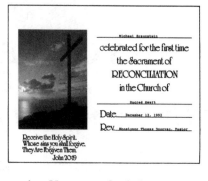

Michael Braunstein
celebrated for the first time
the Sacrament of
RECONCILIATION
in the Church of
Sacred Heart
Date December 12, 1992
Rev. Monsignor Thomas Donovan, Pastor

Receive the Holy Spirit.
Whose sins you shall forgive.
They Are Forgiven Them.
John 20:19

again. You see, God doesn't get mad anymore. He gets hurt.

THE NEW NO-NO'S:
A Thoroughly Modern Catechism

The Joy of Cooking gets updated at least once a decade. So does *Dr. Spock's Baby and Child Care*. Why, then, did it take over four hundred years for the Catholic Church's catechism to get a face-lift? Surely there have been more important changes in Church teachings than in cooking a pot roast or dealing with a colicky baby.

With centuries of change to deal with, the Vatican didn't have any trouble filling almost seven hundred pages of text in its recently published *Universal Catechism*. Fortunately for parochial school-children, the information isn't presented in the *Baltimore Catechism*'s familiar question-and-answer format, so they will not have to tote the weighty volume home from school to memorize questions for tomorrow's religion class. Readers browsing through this trailblazing tome will be comforted to find that all of their favorites—swearing, murder, idolatry, abortion, divorce, extramarital affairs, homosexual behavior, and prostitution—are still sins. Birth control, too, remains taboo when it is systematic and dependable, but not when natural and haphazard.

To reflect modern-day moral temptations, readers will also find a host of new sins, many of which have been deviously lumped under already-recognized sins. Grumbling Catholics might point out that none of the original Ten Commandments have been revoked to compensate for all the new sins. They find the identifying of new offenses all well and good, but object to a net gain of several dozen new sins. At least with the Church's publishing record, they won't have to endure another major change like this in their lifetimes, and nor will their children, grandchildren, great-grandchildren, great-great-grandchildren, or great-great-great-grandchildren.

"Thou shalt not steal" used to be pretty straightforward. With the inclusion of new sins in the seventh-commandment category, Catholics suddenly are not allowed to evade taxes, pay unfair wages, take bribes, forge checks, or swipe a box of paper clips from the company supply room. Modern science is represented in the new catechism with new transgressions condemning genetic engineering. But sinners can choose to be just plain bad or really bad. While donating an egg, sperm,

THE OTHER COMMANDMENTS:
Precepts of the Church

In addition to following the Ten Commandments and the teachings of Christ, Catholics are expected to adhere to a set of regulations popularly known as the Commandments of the Church. Although they originated in the Middle Ages, they have recently been updated, and a seventh commandment has been added to the traditional six.

1. To go to Mass on Sundays and holy days of obligation, and to avoid needless work and business activities on those days.
2. To receive Holy Communion at least once a year between the first Sunday of Lent and Trinity Sunday (the "Easter Duty"), and to receive penance at least once a year, although annual Confession is required only if serious sin is involved.
3. To prepare for Confirmation and to be confirmed.
4. To observe the marriage laws of the Church; to give religious training to your children, and to send them to parish schools or religious education programs.
5. To support the Church, locally and worldwide.
6. To observe the laws of fast and abstinence.
7. To join in the missionary spirit of the Church.

or body to carry a baby is "gravely dishonest," other fertilization techniques such as artificial insemination "are perhaps less worthy of condemnation, but they remain morally unacceptable."

Life-in-the-fast-lane enthusiasts will need to curb their thrills in order to stay in a state

of grace. Drunken driving, smoking in excess, and drug abuse have been added to the lengthy list. New careers are mandatory for fortune-tellers and astrologers who want to remain Good Catholics, since all types of magic, astrology, and clairvoyance are new no-no's. In selecting new professions, these job seekers should not bother to look for work in adult bookstores, as pornographers are now blackballed from heaven.

The new catechism doesn't mention a grace period for the new sins to be brought into effect, so penitence should be in full force all over the Catholic world these days. Surprisingly, there's been no surge in Reconciliation service attendance of late, and confessionals are far from overflowing. We can only assume that new-sin sinners are either piously making their own peace with God or operating in a state of blissful ignorance.

THY PEOPLE SHALL BE MY PEOPLE

The Catholic Wedding

Catholic weddings have not changed much in recent years. Two people still process down the aisle to swear undying love to one another before their family, friends, and God. The ceremony, though, is now a bit more up to date. Catholic couples routinely write their own vows and add personal touches to what once was an unvarying ritual. Certain customs of dubious origin like lighting a "unity candle" or distributing roses to the congregation at the sign of peace have become quite popular. And while you'll still probably hear "Ave Maria," you may also be treated to "The Wedding Song" or even "Tonight's the Night."

But one big thing has changed: who Catholics are marrying. Where once upon a time intermarriage was a rare occurrence, today it's kosher to see a minister or a rabbi up there on the altar with the priest. While in the past interfaith marriages caused consternation and occasionally outright scandal, relatively few relatives are boycotting weddings on religious grounds anymore.

Intermarriage Today

When David raised his foot and stomped down on the glass, a merry roar let loose from the wedding guests. All the guests, that is, except the bride's grandmother, who was clutching her rosary and looking a little bewildered. This kind of true-life scenario is becoming increasingly common as the number of interfaith marriages continues to rise.

These marriages can be divided into two camps: amateur and advanced. The litmus test for telling the difference is whether the non-Catholic partner is a member of a religion that celebrates Christmas. Amateur intermarriages, then, are between Catholics and Protestants. Sure there are differences, but come on, it's all in the family, right? For certain brides and grooms with a laissez-faire attitude toward religion, the differences between their Catholicism and Lutheranism are less important than whether to have the invitations engraved or printed. The prize for the most amateur of all combos: Catholic-Episcopalian marriages.

Advanced intermarriages deserve extra credit. Here are Catholics who have taken the plunge and married Jews, Moslems, Hindus, Buddhists, Shintoists, Parsis, Jains, and Baha'is, not to mention animists,

ancestor worshippers, and people with religions you've never heard of before. In our part of the world, most of these marriages are of the Catholic-Jewish persuasion. Social historians have attempted to document the reasons for the attraction that has led to the increasing number of marriages between Catholics and Jews.

One theory is that guilt attracts guilt, and that the guilt for not going to Mass on Sunday

BUT WHAT ABOUT THE CHILDREN?

Let's take a look at how some Catholic-Jewish couples deal with the religious situations they face.

THE HALF-AND-HALF METHOD: ERIN AND AARON

- Married in a joint ceremony by priest and rabbi. Aaron broke the glass and Erin's sister sang "Ave Maria."
- Decorate their Christmas tree with little Stars of David.
- Teach their children, Elijah and Elizabeth, about both religions so they can pick one when they get older.

THE PAPAL PATH: MARVIN AND MARY

- Mary, a devout Catholic, and Marvin, a not very religious Jew, sign up for pre-Cana conferences. Marvin is prepared to go to post-Cana conferences too if necessary.
- Get married in church, but both of Marvin's parents walk him down the aisle.
- Marvin agrees to raise the children Catholic, but draws the line at any of his daughters becoming nuns.

is not very different from the guilt for eating a bacon cheeseburger. Perhaps it's that non-WASPs have an affinity toward one another, or that the elaborate rules and rituals of the two religions feel familiar and draw a couple together. One of the most popular theories suggests that there is a special chemistry between girls who wore beanies and boys who wear yarmulkes.

THE "TELL 'EM WHAT THEY WANT TO HEAR" APPROACH: SHIRLEY AND PETER

- Before they get married, Peter assures his parents that any children they have will be raised Catholic, and Shirley tells her family that any children will be raised Jewish.
- Much ado about what type of ceremony to have. Solution: Get married by a justice of the peace in a brief civil ceremony.
- Secretly decide to raise their sons Catholic and their daughters Jewish. Complete pandemonium breaks loose in household on all religious holidays.
- Shirley will sell her diary, which details their uproarious religious struggles through the years, to a major movie studio for a cool million.

THE KOSHER WAY: SAL AND SARAH

- Sarah, an observant Jew, and Sal, a lapsed Catholic, marry in synagogue under a chuppah.
- Sal agrees to raise their children Jewish but refuses to attend the Bris if they have boys.
- Their son will be the only Bar Mitzvah boy named Angelo in the history of Temple Beth-El.

II

A
SENTIMENTAL
EDUCATION

THE APPLE DOESN'T FALL FAR FROM THE TREE:
Catholic Grammar School

The desks were pine or Mission-style oak, with a flip top or a curvy piece that encircled you like a loving arm. The blackboard had the Palmer method script above it. Clapping the erasers was a sign of high standing or a punishment, depending on the circumstances. Of course, you had a nun for a teacher.

You lined up in perfectly straight lines before and after class, and there was never any doubt that what you were engaged in was serious business. Your parents scrimped and saved to make sure you had a Catholic education, and you were not—repeat *not!*—allowed to screw it up.

SACRED HEART
SCHOOL
6-2
1992-93
MRS MURNANE

Like a well-trained homing pigeon, you can return in memory to your parochial school experiences of twenty or thirty years ago like they happened yesterday. They defined you spiritually, socially, and personally. To say you were indelibly stamped "Catholic" by them would be an understatement.

Today the atmosphere around the Catholic grammar school has changed considerably. The kids look different: their uniforms are more fashionable; their hair is hipper; they're even allowed to wear jewelry and other adornments—within limits (hoop earrings will never pass muster). Generally, it's hard to tell if you're passing by St. Cecilia's or a posh private school.

Students still line up to go into class every morning, but instead of the orderly, shortest-to-tallest, single-sex queues of the past, any old sort of bunching-up will do. As long as the little bunch doesn't decide to run into the street together, no one seems to get upset by less-than-military precision. Straight lines just don't seem to be as important as they used to be.

Of course they're not. The nuns aren't running the show anymore. Catholic-school teachers are mostly laywomen who look like nuns but aren't. The few nuns who are still in the school look like laywomen. They all seem to have loosened up, the way a dental patient loosens up after a few whiffs of laughing gas. Priests used to come around only to distribute report cards and prizes. Now they can be seen in the playground, wearing jogging shorts and swinging the kids around like a favorite uncle would. Nobody seems to be afraid of anybody anymore.

Discipline remains the keynote, and there are still rules and regulations to break. The difference is that parents once assumed that if Johnny was punished, it was because he had behaved badly and got what he deserved—in fact, he got it again when he got home.

But if a kid gets into trouble today, his parents are going to take his side. "We believe our son," they'll say, even if he's committed a criminal offense. At the tuition they're paying, they want their kids to be stress-free and happy, just like they are at the country club.

CATHOLIC OR PUBLIC, IT'S ALL PLAID TO ME

You pass a school playground filled with laughing children, all neatly dressed in their white shirts and plaid jumpers or navy pants. A typical Catholic school? Guess again. It's one of a small but growing number of public schools that have copied parochial schools and adopted mandatory uniforms for their students.

Maybe those uniforms weren't the most unfashionable things on the planet, but that's what parochial school girls always thought of them. Whether green plaid or blue serge, pleated skirt or bibbed jumper, uniforms were a daily penance to be endured, as was the taunting by the public school girls who seemed to have dozens of stylish school dresses.

But now, all these years later, the score is evened out. The public school uniforms are every bit as ugly as the Catholic ones were. The public school authorities seem to have passed up the beanie, however, a decision understood and applauded by even the most hard-hearted parochial school girl, who wouldn't wish one of those creepy little caps on her worst enemy.

CATHOLIC DIGEST JUNIOR
JUNE 1993

My Most Unforgettable Moment: "I Killed Monsignor Kilkenny"

by Tommy Rinaldi

It was a Tuesday in Lent. I was an altar boy and a basketball player. I decided to go over to the church during the lunch hour to say the Stations of the Cross. The whole school did the Stations every Friday. But that day, I was feeling kind of holy and went on my own.

This was not strictly allowed by the nuns. Several students had seen statues in the Church weeping and moving, so we were confined to the schoolyard during recess. But I thought I couldn't get into that much trouble for praying. As it turned out, there would soon be tears in that church, but it wouldn't be the statues that were crying.

I had gotten to the Third Station. Like other kids, I was totally empathizing with Jesus' suffering. In fact, on Fridays, by "Veronica Wipes the Face of Jesus," all the girls were crying. I wasn't yet, but I was deeply moved. So moved that I didn't notice what must have been the shuffle of Monsignor Kilkenny's ninety-year-old feet as he made his way out of the confessional where he had been napping, as he was wont to do. Evidently, he didn't notice me either, because as I genuflected in front of "Jesus Falls the First Time," he tragically tumbled over my kneeling frame.

Heaven help me. Monsignor never recovered from the injuries he sustained, although he lingered for three days before succumbing. Most Precious Blood put on the biggest extravaganza in its history for his funeral. They took us out of school to go to it, every single kid. Monsignor was laid out at the front of the church in an open coffin. And if that wasn't the scariest thing any of us had ever seen, he was propped up so that wherever you were sitting you were looking right at the face of a dead guy. Some of the first graders have never gotten over the shock.

And neither have I. To this day, I am known in Most Precious Blood parish as The Boy Who Killed Monsignor Kilkenny.

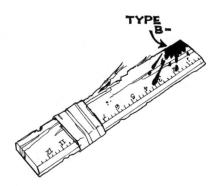

"I Am Sister's Ruler"

I may look like nothing more than a thin piece of wood to you, but I am Sister Mary Ignatius Loyola's most valuable teaching tool. I have been with her for forty years, and although I am retired now, I have had a very active life.

I began my career in a first-grade classroom in a suburb of Philadelphia. It was a good place to start. I only had to wave around in Sister's hand to maintain discipline. Since the little kids were frightened at the sight of me, my other duties were light. Later, I would be tested more strenuously.

I soon found myself patrolling a second-grade class. These kids had reached the age of reason. They were seven, and hardened. They knew the difference between right and wrong, and my job was to keep them honest. When they chose to do wrong, I stepped in. They were a tough bunch. Sometimes they forgot their prayers. Sometimes they left their ties home. Sometimes their homework was sloppily prepared. I think I helped make them better people—and better Catholics.

Sister and I eventually hit the big time. We were seasoned educators and ready to take on a really recalcitrant crowd—the eighth grade at St. Theresa Little Flower of Jesus School in Bryn Mawr. These kids flagrantly violated every rule in the book. They walked down any side of the corridor they felt like. They defaced their textbooks willy-nilly. They smoked in the bathrooms. This was a very demanding time but ultimately the most rewarding stage of my career. I was taxed to the limit. In fact, I incurred a compound fracture while nearly inflicting a compound fracture on a particularly headstrong note-passer. Loyola and I retired soon after that episode. I rest comfortably on her desk in prayerful repose, called into service only to dramatize the most glorious moments of our career.

Humor in Uniform

My parish priest, following the lead of Father Greeley and other priests, has taken to writing novels. Frequently, instead of giving a sermon, Father will discuss the various plot devices he is employing or regale the congregation with the trials of finding a "really good agent," even though he has only two chapters of his novel, *The Ripped Cassock,* in typescript. If this is the best Father can do to contribute to the building fund, the parish had better organize some more bake sales.

—Juan Estevez, Los Angeles

At my Catholic university, all the crucifixes have been removed from the classrooms, since they offended many of the non-Catholics whose tuition now makes up a significant part of the school's operating budget. One priest, however, remains undaunted. He brings his own crucifix to class and with one swift roundhouse, slaps it to the wall behind him—it has its own special sticky tape on the back—and begins teaching class. At the end of his class, he extravagantly rips the crucifix from the wall and stomps out of the room. All the students get the biggest charge out of this.

—Carol Tzcke, Chicago

Sister Joan, my parish's religious education director, has once again been arrested, this time for her sit-in at a nuclear power plant near the parish. This is the fourth time Sister has been arrested this year. There was the ecology rally at the logging company headquarters that got out of hand, the boycott at the pet store where she was arrested for trying to "liberate" a puppy-mill puppy, and of course the storming of the bishop's office—where she sat in the bishop's chair and lit up one of his cigars in a "women are priestly people too" demonstration. On Sunday, the parish takes up a second collection for the Sister Joan Bail Fund.

—Beth Lewis, Seattle

It Pays to Enrich Your Word Power

The language of Catholicism is full of intriguing words that are not often used in everyday life. Circle the word or phrase you believe is *nearest in meaning* to the key word.

1. Transubstantiation
   A. underground railway station
   B. changing bread and wine into the body and blood of Christ
   C. corroboration of evidence
2. Monstrance
   A. type of scary ogre
   B. mystical religious spell
   C. decorative gold contraption used to display a large Communion Host
3. Trespass
   A. take a shortcut through the Sweeneys' backyard
   B. to sin
   C. coupon for free haircut
4. Covet
   A. a down-filled comforter
   B. group of witches
   C. want in an envious or lustful sort of way
5. Hallowed
   A. having an empty hole inside, like a tree
   B. blessed
   C. anything having to do with Halloween
6. Grace
   A. a sanctifying goodness from God
   B. short prayer before a meal
   C. attractive *L.A. Law* attorney
7. Decade
   A. ten years
   B. marked by decay or decline
   C. ten Hail Marys and one Our Father
8. Inculturation
   A. afternoon in a museum
   B. good pearl care
   C. adapting church rituals to local culture

9. Calumny
   A. a cure for mosquito bites
   B. slander
   C. last Roman emperor to persecute Christians
10. Thurible
    A. really, really bad
    B. prayer said only on Thursdays
    C. incense holder

Vocabulary ratings

1–3 correct   Pray for guidance.
4–7 correct   You require remedial catechism class.
8–9 correct   You're probably a CCD teacher. If you're not, you
               should be.
Perfect score Polish your halo.

Answers:
1, B. 2, C. 3, B. 4, C. 5, B. 6, A. 7, C. 8, C. 9, C. 10, C.

Laughter, the Best Medicine

When a nun posed the question "Who is God?" to seven-year-old Anne Marie, she heard the confident reply, "God is the string bean who made all things."

—Maria Sanchez, Cleveland, Ohio

Lively fourth graders at St. Joseph's School in Kansas City play an unspoken game at the class's weekly Mass: the first person to reach the rail to receive Communion wins. In her eagerness, a girl named Patricia scooted up to the altar the moment she heard the bell. Unfortunately, that particular bell signified the offering. Pay attention, Patty!

—Tom White, Tacoma, Washington

A father from Queens, New York, listens to his young son finishing a heartfelt rendition of the Our Father with "and lead us not into Penn Station, but deliver us from evil." And he swears he's never brought the boy into the city.

—Bill Busis, Metuchen, New Jersey

My Trip to Assisi

by Caitlin Kelly, Fifth Grade

St. Francis lived here. So did his girlfriend Clare. St. Francis was not always a saint. He used to be bad, then he got sick and got good. St. Francis liked animals—even the little things that lived in his hair and on his skin. When you're a saint like St. Francis, a dog, a cat, a horse, a flea, a louse, it is all the same to you. Today Assisi is a very good place for stray cats to live. People take care of them in case he is looking. His bones are just down the street in the basement of the church, close enough to keep everyone on their best behavior.

In fact, in Assisi it is hard not to think about St. Francis a lot. People are still going around dressed like him. The church they built for him has a lot of famous paintings in it, but that is not the good part. The good part is the bones, and the robe and the sandals. St. Francis had the stigmata, which means his hands and feet bled like Jesus' did on the cross. Creepy.

There is a garden near Assisi. One time St. Francis was tempted to be bad again so he threw himself on the rosebush in the garden—which is sort of like pinching yourself. But since he was a saint the thorns went away. This rosebush is still there and blooms every May. We were there in August so I didn't see this for myself but I believe it.

St. Clare liked St. Francis a lot, and did whatever he did. St. Clare had visions, so they made her the patron saint of television. You can buy statues of her that have two holes in them for your TV antenna. But no one has an antenna anymore. Maybe they will change her to the patron saint of cable.

A BANQUET IS PREPARED:
First Holy Communion

First Holy Communion today, like just about everything else in the Catholic Church, has an element of choice. Once upon a time, a whole grade received First Holy Communion together. Dressed in white mini bridal dresses and blue or white suits, they marched into church in size order and sat together in the front in strictly assigned places in strictly assigned pews. Families sat at the back like guests at a wedding.

Today, the new communicants—still dressed in traditional attire—are free to receive First Communion the old-fashioned way, or in the company of their families, or solo, at a regular

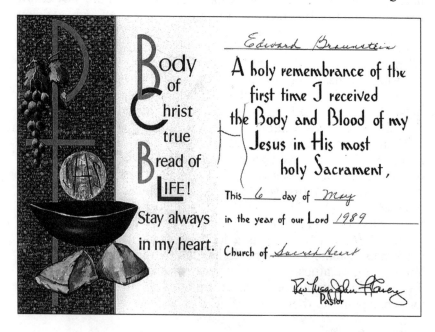

Body
of
Christ
true
Bread of
LIFE!
Stay always
in my heart.

Edward Braunstein

A holy remembrance of the
first time I received
the Body and Blood of my
Jesus in His most
holy Sacrament,

This _6_ day of _May_
in the year of our Lord _1989_

Church of _Sacred Heart_

Rev Msgr John Flavey
Pastor

Mass. It depends on their parish and their own preference. Some kids would rather die than parade up to the altar with Mom and Dad in tow; others feel that the family that receives together, believes together.

Communion parties have really undergone a change as well. Once exclusively an occasion for a modest family party, First Communion celebrations today sometimes approach the lavishness of a wedding or a Bar Mitzvah. Such wingdings come complete with limousines, catering halls, and bands. Kiddies who were once content to run around the house and scream at old-style Communion parties are now entertained by rented ponies or carousels.

THE NAME GAME:

CONFIRMATION

THOMAS BENVENUTO

Receive the Seal
of the Holy Spirit
the Gift of the Father

In the name of the Father +
and of the Son +
and of the holy Spirit +

This _5_ day of _May_ in the year
of our Lord and Savior _1990_
Mater Christi church
Bishop _John McGuire_

The only thing about Confirmation that seems to change from year to year is the names kids try to get away with before Sister or Father or someone makes them take a bona fide saint's name. While years ago children tried to slip names like Lolita or Elvis past Sister Nomenclatura (a little bit like trying to slip an iceberg past the *Titanic*), here are some names today's little Soldiers of Christ would like to select if they could.

Dhilisam	Zangief
Ryu	Chung-li
Guile	Vega
Blanka	Orson
Elmo	Bart

HORMONES AND HAMBURGERS:
The Modern Catholic High School

✝

Like drug dealers and hookers, Catholic high school students today come equipped with beepers. In the case of the students, the beeps generally come from Mom, or so the students say. Once those beeps come in, today's free-range students now have a place to make a call. Where schools once had maybe one pay phone that was hardly ever used (students didn't used to have free time to make calls), the phone banks in a Catholic high school are only slightly smaller than those at the arrival terminal of a mid-size airport.

The kids have also adopted some other bizarre inner-city fashions, like wearing pacifiers around their necks and walking through the halls sucking on them. Apparently, the only thing that distinguishes Catholic high school students from their inner-city counterparts is the ability to pay a high tuition.

Catholic high schools, like their elementary counterparts, are beginning to look like fancy private schools. The cafeteria is one of the first places the change can be observed. Once the no-nonsense dispensary of inedible chow whose only virtue was that it was better than suffering the indignity of bringing your lunch in a paper bag (always the height of uncool), the cafeteria is now a catered affair.

Franchises bid for the opportunity to serve up upmarket breakfasts (yes, breakfasts) and lunches—with a selection rivaling the food court at a mall. The cafeteria, once the bastion of complaint and disgust, is now as popular as McDonald's Moscow. Thanks to the pro caterers, awards banquets, and alumni gatherings have all the style and verve of Oscar-night parties in Hollywood—well, almost. They all have champagne fountains and uniformed waiters and waitresses, at least.

And it isn't only the food service that has gone corporate. The nuns on the faculty run the schools like CEOs—and look the part as well. For many of these briefcase-toting Sisters, being the principal of an affluent Catholic high school is like scoring the Lexus dealership in an elite zip code.

Where once it was thought that the sexes had to be separated by several blocks, a wall or two, and a barbed-wire fence, the school authorities have thrown caution to the wind and consented to coeducation. Yes, some daring schools have taken the plunge and allowed boys and girls to be together in the classroom. Presumably, they've found subtler ways to keep the minds of impressionable young people off their raging hormones. The good old CYO, which performed this function in the past, has been updated. Students can now join clubs like RAP—Religion and People—which sponsors wholesome venues for cruising—um, getting to really know one another as *people*.

SATURDAY NIGHT AT ST. VITUS:
The High School Dance

While Catholic teenagers may not have changed substantially in the last generation or two, the dances they attend certainly have. Formerly demure affairs patrolled by vigilant Sisters on the alert for any signs of misconduct, impurity, or, for that matter, fun, dances are now chaperoned by parents and religious who have to be paid to be there.

Girls and boys still stand around in separate packs. But while the girls have always danced with one another, today the boys do it too. When they finally start to mingle, there's no longer any need for chaperones to tell love-struck couples to leave room between them for the Holy Spirit. Couples don't touch each other very much on the dance floor anymore. Teenagers have found ways of dancing that make the lambada look subtle, but the chaperones hardly raise an eyebrow. They are more concerned with stopping fights and controlling the overexuberant slam-dancing of high-spirited youngsters. If things get too rough, they can call for backup from the cops parked outside.

"I HAD THIS NUN . . .":
Favorite Nun Stories

Mary Gallo, Queens, New York. I had this nun in the third grade who had been telling us all year about what a horrible person Khrushchev was. He didn't believe in God and he wanted to take over the United States. During the Cuban Missile Crisis her predictions became more and more dire. On the day the crisis peaked, we said our prayers and then Sister Dolorosa told us that Khrushchev was going to blow the world up, probably today. She said we had to be sure to hurry home after school to say goodbye to our parents. In a panic, I ran home at lunch and threw myself hysterically at my mother, begging her to call Daddy at work and tell him to come home before it was too late. My father reassured me that the world was not likely to come to an end that day. When the following morning dawned after all, my mother had her own little blow-up with Sister Dolorosa.

Frances Schmidt, Philadelphia. I was a pretty rebellious kid in high school who got a kick out of breaking the rules, particularly when it came to my uniform. We had a very strict dress code that called for—among other things—blue knee socks and brown loafers. One day I wore black hightops. Before I had my coat in my locker, Sister Vigilanta swooped over and said to me, "Miss Schmidt, your sneakers tell me you don't care." I told her I didn't know they could talk. I spent the next two weeks in detention.

Patty McGonigle, Cleveland. I went to a very staid all-girls high school with a very boring uniform that I tried to jazz up in any way I could. We had to wear white shirts, gray pleated skirts, and blue blazers. In an imaginative moment, I asked my mother to knit me a blue, white, and gray argyle vest. On the first day I wore it, I was called to the principal's office. Sister Minutiae told me that I was allowed to wear (1) a blue vest; (2) a white vest; (3) a gray vest; (4) a blue and white vest; (5) a gray and white vest; or (6) a gray and blue vest. But I was definitely not allowed to wear a blue, white, *and* gray vest.

Carol Zawicki, Chicago. I attended Marywood Academy, a school with great aspirations to gentility. Before every vacation, we were asked to polish our wooden desks using a product called Pride. One year, just before we went home for Christmas vacation, there came an announcement over the intercom from Sister Immaculata: "Would anyone who has any pride left please report to the principal's office?"

Lorrie Garofolo, San Francisco. Sister Concepción, the geriatric health ed nun at Holy Family High School, was scheduled to tell us about sexually transmitted diseases. She came into the class holding two pamphlets. I could see that one said "Gonorrhea" on the cover; the other said "Syphilis." She held one up and said, "This is this." Then she held the other one up and said, "And this is this." End of lecture.

Anne Lynch, Houston. Sister Debilitata, our French teacher in senior year at St. Dymphna's, was having a difficult

time. She was so nervous in front of the class that at times she could hardly speak, let alone *parler*. It was clear to one and all, including Sister, that her grip on reality was tenuous. We took full advantage. One day, one of the girls brought in a clicker, the kind ordinarily used by nuns to call the class to order. She clicked it several times, and as Sister rushed over in alarm, the girl passed it on, so that the next click came from a different part of the room. The class kept a completely straight face. After several repeats of this, Sister was convinced that she was the only one who had heard the noises. That class was the last we saw of her. Eventually, we were told that Sister had gone away. I suppose if this were being made into a movie, it would be called *Driving Sister Crazy*.

Paul Harrigan, Detroit. I never got to school on time in high school. I started every day staring down Sister Punctilius in the late office. She was a scary-looking thing—tall, gaunt, and ancient. "Do I look like a mean old, rotten, vindictive old shrew?" she'd growl. Of course she did. "No, Sister," I'd dutifully reply, afraid she was reading my mind. Then she'd lean over, look me straight in the face, and hiss, "Well, I *am!*" I learned to respect her.

Kate Capelli, Kansas City, Missouri. Sister Horribila, my favorite fourth-grade nun, warned us not to do two things: tease our hair or drink out of public water fountains. If you wore big teased hair (which we weren't going to do in fourth grade anyway), bugs would drop in it, build their nests, and have babies in your hair. She knew someone it happened to. And if you drank from public water fountains you could swallow a snake egg, which would hatch in your stomach and grow. The snake would have to climb up your throat to get out. She knew someone it happened to. The doctors had to put trays of food in front of the woman so the snake would smell it and come out. But when the snake began to come out, a nurse got so scared she screamed. The snake bit the lady and she died. Sister knew someone it happened to, of course, although no one else ever did.

✝
THESE FOOLISH THINGS REMIND ME OF YOU:

WHAT WE MISS ABOUT NUNS

Today's nun is, as often as not, an uptown woman, thumbing her Filofax for her next appointment, stopping by the manicurist to fix a broken nail on her way to a lunch date, then dashing back to work. She dresses stylishly, though her wardrobe may contain a few more navy-blue outfits than the national average. A cross around the neck used to be a surefire way to tell a nun from a non, but that test is no longer entirely reliable. You have to look closely to see the pin on her lapel.

But it's not appearance alone that sets present-day nuns apart from their sisters of yore. The real difference is that today's nuns aren't scary, which makes them a whole new breed. With a residual anxiety that has been tempered by the passing years, many Catholics look at nuns differently today. They feel privileged to have been taught by some of these extraordinary women, and fondly remember the little things they remember about nuns—things their children will never know.

Their eyeglasses	Their "wedding" rings
Their soapy scent	Their soft hands
Their smooth skin	Their deep pockets
Their starched habits	Their calm voices
Their scrubbed faces	Their fountain pens
Their flowing skirts	Their names
Their shoes	Their handwriting
Their pitch pipes	The creases in their veils
Their wraps	

THE EVOLUTION OF NUNS

THEY'VE GOT WHAT IT TAKES:

WOMEN WHO COULD HAVE BEEN NUNS

Barbara Bush	Hillary Rodham Clinton
Ann B. Davis	Julie Andrews
Donna Shalala	Jean Harris
Anne Murray	Dianne Feinstein
Anita Hill	Mary Tyler Moore
Joanne Woodward	Barbara Jordan
Jeane Kirkpatrick	Miss Jane Hathaway
Donna Reed	Marilyn Quayle

WOMEN WHO COULD NEVER HAVE BEEN NUNS

Nancy Reagan	Raquel Welch
Demi Moore	Whitney Houston
Jane Fonda	Brigitte Bardot
LaToya Jackson	Paula Abdul
Sean Young	Marge Schott
Whoopi Goldberg	Aretha Franklin
k. d. lang	Barbra Streisand

HOW CATHOLIC IS IT?:
Catholic Colleges Today

Catholic colleges just don't seem to be quite as Catholic as they used to be. There aren't as many priests, brothers, and nuns teaching in them, for one thing, and religious education has been deemphasized. Meanwhile, the social life of students at Catholic colleges—once known for their strict discipline and rigorous moral code—now resembles that of students at non-Catholic schools. In fact, it's getting pretty hard to tell if a college is Catholic.

But there are two big clues. The school's name is usually, but not always, a dead giveaway. And a whole lot of the students are Catholic.

Here are the Top Fifteen—the colleges with the most Catholic student bodies.

1. Boston College, Chestnut Hill, Massachusetts
2. Catholic University of America, Washington, D.C.
3. De Paul University, Chicago, Illinois
4. Fairfield University, Fairfield, Connecticut
5. College of the Holy Cross, Worcester, Massachusetts
6. Iona College, New Rochelle, New York
7. Loyola University in New Orleans, New Orleans, Louisiana
8. Loyola University of Chicago, Chicago, Illinois
9. Manhattan College, Riverdale, New York
10. University of Notre Dame, Notre Dame, Indiana
11. Providence College, Providence, Rhode Island
12. St. Bonaventure University, St. Bonaventure, New York
13. College of St. Catherine, St. Paul, Minnesota
14. St. John's University, Jamaica, New York
15. Villanova University, Villanova, Pennsylvania

Here's how some of the others stack up according to percentage of Catholics on campus.

Fordham University, New York, New York (85%)

St. Norbert College, De Pere, Wisconsin (84%)

University of Scranton, Scranton, Pennsylvania (83%)

Duquesne University, Pittsburgh, Pennsylvania (80%)

St. John's University, Collegeville, Minnesota (78%)

University of Dayton, Dayton, Ohio (77%)

Loyola College, Baltimore, Maryland (76%)

Lewis University, Romeoville, Illinois (75%)

La Salle University, Philadelphia, Pennsylvania (75%)

Niagara University, Niagara University, New York (70%)

John Carroll University, Cleveland, Ohio (70%)

University of St. Thomas, St. Paul, Minnesota (70%)

University of Dallas, Irving, Texas (69%)

Rockhurst College, Kansas City, Missouri (68%)

Marquette University, Milwaukee, Wisconsin (66%)

Loyola Marymount University, Los Angeles, California (65%)

St. Louis University, St. Louis, Missouri (64%)

Gonzaga University, Spokane, Washington (62%)

Creighton University, Omaha, Nebraska (61%)

University of San Diego, San Diego, California (61%)

University of Santa Clara, Santa Clara, California (61%)

Mercyhurst College, Erie, Pennsylvania (61%)

Canisius College, Buffalo, New York (60%)

Marist College, Poughkeepsie, New York (60%)

Gannon University, Erie, Pennsylvania (59%)

Georgetown University, Washington, D.C. (58%)

Regis University, Denver, Colorado (54%)

Marymount University, Arlington, Virginia (46%)

University of Portland, Portland, Oregon (45%)

Xavier University of Louisiana, New Orleans, Louisiana (44%)

University of San Francisco, San Francisco, California (40%)

Christian Brothers University, Memphis, Tennessee (32%)

CATHOLIC ART HISTORY 101

Le Moyne College, Syracuse,   New York (85%)

Many young Catholics study the history of art in college, snoozing through carousels of slides just like every other art history student in the world. What these future patrons of the arts may not realize is that many paintings have an elusive religious context or suggestive

quirk that won't be mentioned in their textbooks. For their erudition: *MAESTA, Duccio (1278–1319)*. If you think you're tired of seeing pictures of Madonna now, you should have lived during the Middle

Ages, when *the* Madonna was portrayed by everyone who had a paint-brush—over the course of several *centuries*. Note the graceful pose of this typical Madonna, the rich folds of fabric in her gown, and the tender, melancholy expression on her face. When you get down to it, all you need to know about this painting—and virtually all medieval Christian art—is that no one smiles and the Baby Jesus always looks like a miniature adult.

ANNUNCIATION, Fra Angelico (1400–55). This evocative painting is by the Dominican friar Guido di Pietro. Although history doesn't specifically say why he was nicknamed "the angelic friar," critics believe the name may first have emerged about the time he gave up painting to tend the vineyards and develop Frangelico, the hazelnut liqueur. In this work, the Madonna's usually serene expression is not altered by what must have been the surprise of her life.

THE LAST SUPPER, Leonardo da Vinci (1452–1519). Yes, the dynamic perspective and psychological content make up an expressive unity, but the eternal question remains open to scholarly

The Last Supper

debate: Why is everyone sitting on the same side of the table?
ECSTASY OF ST. THERESA, Giovanni Lorenzo Bernini (1598–1680).
The ecstasy in which St. Theresa seems to be writhing is suppos-
edly a spiritual one. This interpretation has produced uncontrol-

lable laughter in generations of Catholic school girls.

SUNDAY AFTERNOON ON THE ISLAND OF LA GRANDE JATTE, Georges Seurat (1859–91). The luminous new technique of pointillism used by Seurat contrasts with the plaintive, brooding expressions of his subjects. Why this provocative juxtaposition? Scholars surmise that the French picnickers skipped Mass to spend a leisurely day in the park and later felt guilty about it.

THE FACADE OF ROUEN CATHEDRAL, Claude Monet (1840–1926). Degas painted horse races and ballet dancers, and Renoir was famous for his paintings of pretty women and children, but Monet diverged from those Impressionist themes. He is best known for being the only Impressionist to paint churches.

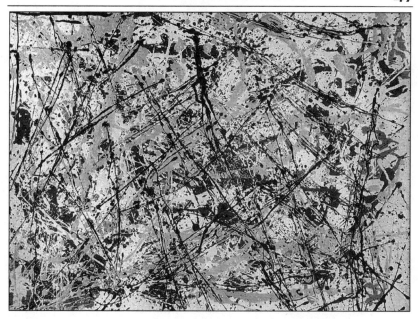

UNTITLED, Jackson Pollock (1912– 56). They say God is everywhere.

III

WE
GATHER
TOGETHER

THE CHURCH NEXT DOOR:
The Basic Suburban Parish

Just like the boy next door, this parish is familiar, comfortable, and all-American. The life of the basic suburban parish revolves around family, kids, and the parish school. But also like the boy next door, it's not as ordinary as you might assume.

Who would expect families with such nice front lawns to care so much about the less fortunate? But at SS. Peter and Paul, the sign-up sheet for sleep-over and cleanup duty at the parish homeless shelter is filled for months ahead. And who would expect such a backwater to have embraced liturgical changes Rome is still in a dither over? Conservative as SS. Peter and Paul may seem to be, it's not at all uncommon to go to Mass there and find altar girls or women serving Communion *in flagrante delicto*.

SS. Peter and Paul is where the next generation of Catholics is being propagated. A week in this church gives you a real slice of contemporary Catholic life—there are births and baptisms, weddings and funerals. Over the course of a year there are abundant milestones—First Communions, Confirmations, graduations. In most parishes like this, a handful of priests are serving huge numbers of parishioners. The Mass schedule is as crowded as a rush-hour train timetable, and Mass is as crowded as the train.

So if you're wondering where all those Catholics you thought stopped going to Mass years ago can be found, try looking for them at the 10:15 next Sunday at the church next door.

THE ON-LINE CHURCH:
Parochial Software

Like virtually every other institution in today's society, churches have moved firmly into the computer age. There are even special software packages tailored specifically to their needs. One of the most popular is PowerChurch Plus®, whose advertising brochure invites church administrators to "Unleash the Power!"

With this software, parishes can keep close tabs on membership and finances—perhaps a little too close for some people's tastes. For example, the new software can print out reports telling exactly when a parishioner did and did not attend Mass, as well as precisely how much he or she put in the collection basket. Parishes can also program their computers to spit out automatic reminders, just like those annoying "past due" and "about to expire" notices we all occasionally receive. One series of notices might go something like this:

First notice
We notice you haven't been to Mass this Easter season and remind you that the Church requires that you receive Holy Communion at least once during this period. You are a valued member of our parish community, and we hope to see you soon.

Second notice
Have we done anything to offend you? We sincerely hope not, and remind you that Father Leo is always available to discuss any difficulties you may be having with the Church or in your personal life. We urgently remind you that there are only two Sundays left for you to make your Easter Duty. Please disregard this notice if you have already received.

Third notice
We're very sorry. Our records indicate that you are no longer in a state of grace, despite our best efforts. Please call the parish office at your earliest opportunity to schedule a Reconciliation with Father Leo—and do drive carefully until then.

✝
THE WELL-ROUNDED PARISH:

MINISTRIES AND SERVICES

AIDS Pastoral Ministry
AlcoholicsAnonymous/Al-Anon
All Night Vigil
Altar Rosary Society
Bereavement Support Group
Bread of Life Food Pantry
Catholic Charismatic Prayer
    Group
Daily Exposition of the
    Blessed Sacrament

Fatima Blue Army Cell Prayer
    Group
Mother of Perpetual Help
    Novena
Over-40 Singles Group
Padre Pío Prayer Group
Prayer Garden
Sexaholics Anonymous
Spiritual Direction Ministry

WHEREVER TWO OR MORE ARE GATHERED TOGETHER:
Catholic Associations

You can find the Nocturnal Adoration Society, the Mothers' Club, or the Knights of Columbus at any old parish. Here are some other Catholic extracurricular groups that you may have to look a little harder to find.

American Catholic Correctional
    Chaplains Association
American Friends of the Vatican
    Library
Apostleship of the Sea
Catholic Golden Age
Catholic One Parent Organization
Catholic Order of Foresters
Czech Catholic Union of Texas
Damien-Dutton Society for
    Leprosy Aid
First Catholic Slovak Ladies
    Association, U.S.A.
Free the Fathers

Frontier Apostolate
Maryheart Crusaders
National Association of Priest Pilots
National Catholic Bandmasters'
    Association
National Catholic Cemetery
    Conference
National Catholic Conference of
    Airport Chaplains
National Catholic Forensic League
National Catholic Pharmacists' Guild
Philangeli (Friends of the Angels)
St. Gregory Foundation for Latin
    Liturgy

THE BEST LITTLE LITURGY IN TOWN:
The Progressive Urban Parish

The progressive urban parish combines an enthusiasm for the reforms of Vatican II, a sense of tradition, and a strong concern for social justice. Soup kitchens and homeless shelters are *de rigueur,* while the parish hall is filled from morning till night with every twelve-step group except Recovering Catholics. Official prohibitions against female altar persons, eucharistic ministers, and homilists are blithely ignored.

Frequently a sanctuary for liberal Catholics, the progressive urban parish nevertheless treasures the Church's beautiful old rituals. Mass here features a full choir which performs the most exquisite church music of the ages. There are plenty of rousing old hymns, for those who despaired of ever again singing "Holy God, We Praise Thy Name," "For All the Saints," or "Crown Him with Many

Crowns." And asthmatics beware: clouds of incense are generated on the slightest liturgical pretext, setting off rounds of discreet coughing and eye-wiping throughout the church. In short, the progressive urban parish is not a place where people attend Mass to "get it over with." It tends to be jammed on the holidays—not only with regular parishioners but with refugees from less spirited parishes.

Progressive urban parishes are often housed in grand old churches that were built a cen-

tury ago by the grandparents of the people now sitting in the pews. These churches have been lovingly restored, frequently with the help of volunteers from the congregation. Many of the volunteers, along with a fair number of the parishioners in general, are confirmed bachelors. Perhaps this accounts for the presence of a Fabric Committee, along with the usual Liturgy Committee and Parish Council, on the official roster of at least one parish in New York City's Greenwich Village.

MORE CATHOLIC THAN THE POPE:
Our Friends the Episcopalians

Do you miss incense? Long church processions? Organ music? Stop by your local Episcopalian church. Although Episcopalian services vary somewhat from "high church" to "low church," the high variety looks an awful lot like the old Roman Catholic Mass. Yet there are major differences between Episcopalian and Catholic liturgies—starting with female bishops, priests, and deacons.

Perhaps for this reason, it

comes as a surprise to many Catholics that the 'Piskies (and Lutherans too!) say the same Creed that we do. In fact, our Anglican cousins consider themselves to be part of the "one holy, catholic, and apostolic church"—but that's catholic with a small *c*.

Of course, Roman Catholics will never quite forgive the Episcopalians for breaking away. But they do admire Episcopalian good taste. Let's face it, their grandparents, like George Bush's, had more money and education than ours. And they've done a neat job of modernizing their Church without throwing out some of the best ancient rituals, as many Catholics accuse our own Church of doing.

Still, many Catholics view Episcopalians with spiritual condescension. Possibly this has something to do with the fact that an Anglican bishop in England publicly questioned the divinity of Christ a few years back. Or maybe it's because Episcopalian churches have been known to serve sherry for a dollar after their Masses. Deep down, Catholics suspect that Episcopalians love the show, but waffle on the bed-rock issues.

In days past, priests and nuns had little scope for self-expression in their free time. They seemed to be confined, for the most part, to visiting their sick and elderly parents, going on retreat, or taking other people on retreat. Today's priests and nuns suffer under no such strictures, enjoying a much wider range of activities.

THINGS PRIESTS DO ON THEIR DAY OFF

1. Go to the gym
2. Visit vacation condo
3. Add to Hummel collection
4. Play golf
5. Eat out
6. Go to the theater
7. Hang out with friends
8. Go to ball games
9. Rent movies
10. Test-drive sports cars

THINGS NUNS DO ON THEIR DAY OFF

1. Go shopping
2. Grade papers
3. Watch TV
4. Visit friends
5. Jog
6. Read
7. Sew
8. Go to the movies
9. Volunteer at the home-less women's shelter
10. Go to Vegas

DEACONS: PRIESTS' PROXIES

In an age when there aren't enough priests to go around, the Church has seen fit to send in substitutes: pastoral associates and deacons. In some parishes that lack priests altogether, pastoral associates (many of them nuns) see to the day-to-day running of the parish and fulfill many of the obligations of the pastor. Permanent deacons are men who are rigorously trained and solemnly deputized to fill in for priests in all but a few instances.

WHAT DEACONS CAN'T DO

1. Absolve sins
2. Administer the Sacrament of the Sick
3. Consecrate the Eucharist

WHAT DEACONS CAN DO

1. Read the Gospel at Mass
2. Give sermons
3. Distribute Communion
4. Perform marriages
5. Baptize
6. Conduct interments
7. Be married

SOMETHING OLD, SOMETHING NEW:
What to Get Your Priest for His Wedding

A recent Gallup poll found that 75 percent of American Catholics support the idea of a married priesthood. What might happen if the Vatican finally relented and allowed priests to marry? Imagine the following scene.

Well, that blessed day has finally arrived. Your best friend, confidant, and mentor will finally be tying the knot. You fully realize that this means you will be seeing less of him. No more lingering chats after the Building Fund Picnic, no more late night calls to talk over the day's events, and no more hushed discussions of Father Greeley's latest plot line.

No, your best pal will have not only his priestly duties but his marital ones as well.

You have made this adjustment before for other friends, and you will make it for him. But what to get the holy couple . . . Here are some of the most popular items at the gift table of the most chic priestly weddings.

Sterling-silver Roman collar pin
The Joy of Sex
Itty-bitty book light for late night sermon writing without waking up spouse
Matching wine, vinegar, and oil cruets
Franciscan china
Black linens

OUR PARENT, WHO ART IN HEAVEN:
How to Be Liturgically Correct

A religious version of Political Correctness is gaining ground among many Catholics. They want to be Liturgically Correct, or L.C. One goal of the L.C. movement is to eliminate sexist language from Catholic prayers and rituals. Another is to make the meanings of these prayers and rituals more clear by expressing them in modern language.

There's a proposed new L.C. translation of the Mass that's raising the hackles of conservative bishops, starting with Cardinal Roger Mahony of Los Angeles. The good cardinal doesn't want the new Mass to drop any references to God the Father.

There are a few basic realities in this L.C. business that

can't be ignored. After all, Jesus was a man. He sometimes referred to God as His Father. And the greatest mysteries of human existence are best expressed in rich poetic imagery, not flat, overly literal L.C. prose. But there's no reason to cling to outdated or highfalutin' language for its own sake.

There are some who think that the Vatican has already gone quite far enough by allowing U.S. Catholics to drop "men" from the phrase "who died for us and for all men" in the Creed. On the other side, there are those who won't be happy until every "He" and "Him" is changed to "God" in every ancient hymn (hyrm?).

The following list of terms should be helpful to Catholics who want to be as L.C. as possible:

Non-L.C.	L.C.
Mankind	Humanity; all
Brothers	Brothers and sisters
Father	Parent
Son	Child
He	God; the One
Him	God
Lord	God; Holy One
Christ	God; Jesus
His	God's
Thy	Your
Thine	Yours

YOU SAY MASS, I SAY LITURGY:
A Post–Vatican II Dictionary

Catholics of the old school or those who haven't been to church in a while may be a bit put off by some of the terminology used in the modern Church. The following is a list of some of the more unfamiliar terms and their meanings.

Altar server. Inclusive language, please. In fact, in many dioceses the servers are girls as well as boys, despite Vatican opposition to females on the altar.

Community. A buzzword often used in the more progressive parishes. Much effort is expended to turn the parish into a "community" with a real sense of togetherness.

Consensus. How feminists and the Japanese make decisions. Basically, talking everything through until a decision is reached that everyone can live with. First gained a toehold in the Catholic Church among women's religious orders. Recommended for particularly ornery parish councils.

Hierarchy. The top leaders of the Church, especially Vatican officials and the Pope, whom you see as being either hopelessly out of touch or beleaguered defenders of the faith. Formerly referred to as "Rome."

Homily. This term is generally preferred to "sermon" these days. Although they mean just about the same thing, homily implies a closer reliance on scripture. Sermon implies old-fashioned moralizing, which is no longer fashionable.

Liturgy. Does anyone in the trendier parishes say "Mass" anymore? From the Greek, liturgy means literally "the work of the people." This explains why it has been adopted with such enthusiasm by those devoted to the reforms of Vatican II. Still, it strikes many as a bit pretentious. Can you imagine a twelve-year-old running off to make the 5:30 Saturday "liturgy" after baseball practice?

Minister. No, the Protestants have not taken over the rectories. Practically everyone who takes part in the Mass is considered a minister now, including the priest, those who serve Communion, and the musicians.

Preside. Do not tell a committed post–Vatican II priest that you particularly enjoy the way he celebrates Mass. He will answer, "The People of God celebrate Mass. I merely preside."

Sexism. Pronounced a sin by the American bishops in early drafts of their as-yet-unfinished pastoral letter on women, but dropped from later drafts. Conservative Catholics claimed that the bishops were "inventing a sin." It would be comforting to think that the bishops could "uninvent" sexism as easily as they uninvented the sin.

LET US GO TO THE HOUSE OF THE LORD:
Church Architecture

Feel ultra-hip this Sunday? Or perhaps you'd rather have some old-fashioned solitude in which to meditate? Today many cities offer an amazing array of church styles to suit the temperament of every churchgoer. So if you're in no mood for your usual parish church, hop in the car and investigate some of your city's possibilities.

The Outdated Modern: St. Jude's

Like other suburban churches built within the past twenty to thirty years, St. Jude's boasts an architectural style that at the time was cutting-edge modern. Now it is simply dated, with none of the retro charm that has given some older churches a second lease on life. Nonetheless, St. Jude's is as comfy as an old loafer, and will always have its fans.

Pros

Wide aisles, cushioned kneelers, plenty of missalettes.

Original saplings planted on church grounds have grown to create
nicely wooded setting.

Cons

Parishioners beginning to be embarrassed by earnest felt banners
hung behind altar.

Electronic chimes sounding a little tinny these days.

The New Age: St. Gaudi's

Is it a church or a jumbo-size modern sculpture? Newcomers to
St. Gaudi's parish aren't sure at first, but they soon acclimate
themselves to the novel architectural style that their church, and
only their church, has to offer.

Pros

The parish wine bar beats coffee 'n' doughnuts any day.

Meditation in place of homily at Sunday Mass.

Cons

Conservative parishioners dislike contemplative trances that end
weekly Reconciliation service.

Decorative neon distracts the pious from prayer.

The Cathedral: Notre Dame

It's old, it's cavernous, maybe it even has a few poured-concrete gargoyles lurking in the turrets. Whether it's officially a cathedral or just feels like one, Notre Dame, like its counterpart in Paris, is the city's most hallowed place of worship for Catholics.

Pros
You feel a bit more holy whether you are or not.
Easy to feel anonymous in capacious setting.

Cons
Ancient heating system inefficient in winter cold.
Watch out for splinters when sitting in pews.

The Fix-it Fantasy: St. Joseph's

Last year the roof was close to caving in. This year severe structural damage necessitates months of work. Repairs at St. Joseph's have lasted so long that parishioners have gotten used to attending Mass in the parish hall. No matter how much church styles change, this one will always be part of the scenery.

Pros

Standing-room-only conditions inspire a close-knit sense of parish community.

Grateful parish schoolchildren rejoice when Stations of the Cross get cancelled.

Cons

A few defections to nearby St. Anne's parish.

With school gym adjoining parish hall, basketball dribbling drills occasionally disrupt prayer.

BRING FLOWERS OF THE FAIREST:
The Decorative Art of Church Flower Arranging

In days past, a host of dedicated church ladies regularly took charge of arranging flowers for the altar. Often using a hodgepodge of donated funeral flowers, the ladies exercised their creativity with a vengeance. As a result, Mass-goers were typically treated to spikes of orange gladioli radiating outward from a garish center of zinnias and mums, filled out by a few ferns. Holidays and holy days warranted special arrangements, with Easter lilies, palm fronds, or poinsettias in red foil-wrapped pots gracing the altar.

But in the modern parish, where budgets are tight and most of the "ladies" have gone to work, it's not the semi-pro Ladies' Guild that decorates the church anymore. Like many other things these days, church flower arranging has become a catch-as-catch-can enterprise. Harried volunteers have brought new concepts to the art, choosing flowers that sometimes reflect the sensibilities of their fellow parishioners better than the extravaganzas of old.

Here are examples from a few parishes.

Parish Name Theme

There's nothing like roses to remind St. Rose of Lima parishioners of their patroness. Unfortunately, roses are among the most expensive of flowers. This year's eighth-grade class is an artistic one, however, and the children have become adept at making paper roses from gaily colored tissue paper. Huge bouquets of roses now adorn the altar and side chapels. Best of all, they don't need watering!

Less Is More

The subtle Japanese arrangements of ikebana bring a contemplative asceticism that does not go unappreciated by St. Ignatius Loyola parish, whose namesake's order, the Jesuits, brought Catholicism to Japan. The spare look of a few twigs and lotus blossoms provides a restful atmosphere in which to examine one's conscience or work off a penance. With only a few blooms needed, ikebana is economical, too.

Au Naturel

Because St. Fiacre parish is saving up for a new church roof, it is adhering to a strict budget that leaves few funds available for flowers. Enter the faithful team of green-thumbed volunteers, who nevertheless wish to honor the spirit of the saint their parish was named after, the patron of gardeners. They bring in armfuls of tulips, daisies, roses, marigolds, and lavender from their home gardens and place them around the church in an eclectic assortment of vases. So far, no one has missed the orange gladioli.

SING A NEW SONG:

CONTEMPORARY CATHOLIC CHURCH MUSIC

As anyone who has heard the funky version of "Hail Holy Queen Enthroned Above" in the movie *Sister Act* can attest, even the most traditional church music can be made to sound very hip indeed. In fact, the last twenty-five years have seen an explosion of contemporary music written specifically for the Mass. Like a good Broadway musical, the best of it leaves the congregation humming the tunes.

If you're a regular churchgoer, you'll be able to match the titles of some of the most popular contemporary hymns with lines from their texts.

Song Title

1. "On Eagle's Wings"
2. "Be Not Afraid"
3. "Here I Am, Lord"
4. "(Yahweh, I Know) You Are Near"
5. "City of God"
6. "Blest Be the Lord"
7. "One Bread, One Body"
8. "Prayer of St. Francis"
9. "Gift of Finest Wheat"
10. "Come to the Water"
11. "We Are Many Parts"
12. "For You Are My God"
13. "We Have Been Told"
14. "Seek Ye First"
15. "We Walk by Faith"

Lyrics

A. "You satisfy the hungry heart"
B. "And not by sight"
C. "We've seen His Face"
D. "Make me a channel of Your peace"
E. "You alone are my joy"
F. "O let all who thirst"
G. "The Kingdom of God"
H. "We are all one body"
I. "I go before you always"
J. "Standing always at my side"
K. "Is it I, Lord?"
L. "The God of mercy, the God who saves"
M. "One Lord of all"
N. "And He will raise you up"
O. "May our tears be turned into dancing"

Answers:

1, N. 2, I. 3, K. 4, J. 5, O. 6, L. 7, M. 8, D. 9, A. 10, F. 11, H. 12, E. 13, C. 14, G. 15, B.

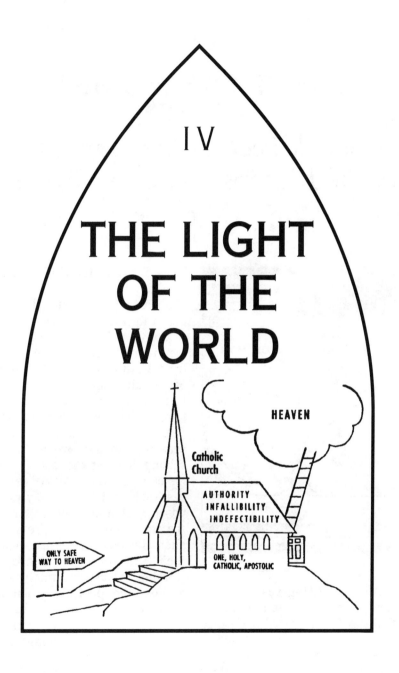

I V

THE LIGHT OF THE WORLD

HEAVEN

Catholic
Church

AUTHORITY
INFALLIBILITY
INDEFECTIBILITY

ONLY SAFE
WAY TO HEAVEN

ONE, HOLY,
CATHOLIC, APOSTOLIC

WHAT DO WOMEN WANT?:

A Sneak Peek at the Final Draft of the Bishops' Letter on Women

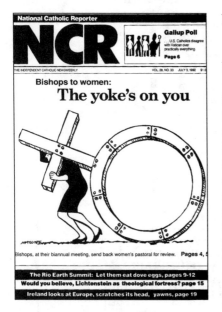

have finally decided to do:

Nothing.

So it is back to the drawing board for the crosier set.

Many issues that directly affect more than half the country's Catholics were the focus of the first four drafts of the bishops' letter. Should there be female lectors, deacons, eucharistic ministers, and altar servers? Should women stop sewing holy statue cozies and instead use their MBAs to invest their parishes' money more wisely? Should they put away the irons they use to press the altar linens and start using their real-world experience as workers, wives, and mothers to address the pressing social issues facing the Church today?

The first draft of the letter offered a ground-breaking new way to view the role of women in the Church. But a funny thing happened as each draft underwent the careful examination of

After nine long years, countless discussions, and more infighting than is found backstage at the Miss Universe pageant, America's bishops have produced four drafts of their much-anticipated "letter on women," and here is what they the bishops. Here, along with an advance look at the upcoming fifth draft, is the changing language of the bishops' letter.

First Draft, 1988
We think it is high time to begin to examine whether or not women may assume the role of priests. There seem to be ample historical and theological grounds for such an examination. Women should definitely be allowed to become deacons, lectors, and altar servers. This would add an entirely new dimension to our liturgy.

Second Draft, 1990
Perhaps we spoke too hastily.

Women and their role in today's Church should be studied carefully. The Church cannot squander the tremendous resources offered by one half of its members.

Third Draft, April 1992
The issue of which liturgical ministries are appropriate for women—short of the priesthood itself, of course—is a conundrum of such complexity that more study is needed.

Fourth Draft, September 1992
This whole "women thing"!

Fifth Draft, 1994
Women are people too.

⚸

THERE SHE IS:

ALTAR GIRLS

Who lights the candles and rings the bells at Mass and wears sneakers under an ill-fitting cassock? If you answered altar boys, you're only partially correct. In some parishes, altar girls now serve as well, a custom that has resulted in reactions ranging from liturgical outrage to a sense of righteous justification.

Several years ago, American bishops asked the Vatican for permission to use female servers, but the request was either eaten by the papal dog or jettisoned to the Pope's back burner; it has never been granted or denied. Without papal permission, bishops have been taking it upon themselves to decide one way or another for their dioceses.

Why all the fuss about altar girls? Who's better qualified to wait on men, wash dishes, wear a dress, smell nice, and keep quiet?

HAIL MARY:
Blessed Among Women

Mary is far and away the most important woman in the Catholic Church or, for that matter, in any major religion. Until Vatican II came along, she had almost equal status with Jesus in the Catholic popular imagination. In fact, her fame is such that, like Madonna and Cher, she gets by with just her first name.

Pope John Paul II is one of Mary's biggest fans, and had a golden "M" emblazoned on his coat of arms when he became a bishop. He prays to the Blessed Virgin often, convinced that she is responsible for saving his life when a gunman shot him at St. Peter's Square in 1981. The assassination attempt took place on May 13, the precise anniversary of the first time Mary appeared at Fatima.

Is she an exalted woman or a symbol of feminine subservience? While the debate rages on, one thing is certain: she is the most venerated woman ever to have lived. Mary is responsible for numerous major feast days and no fewer than three of the six Holy Days of Obligation in the United States: the Solemnity of Mary, Mother of God, January 1; the Assumption of the Blessed Virgin Mary, August 15; and the Immaculate Conception, December 8. Whether by wearing Miraculous Medals, attending Our Mother of Perpetual Help devotions, or simply bowing their heads in prayer, millions of Catholics invoke the name of the Blessed Virgin every day.

WOMEN
OF SUBSTANCE:
Commanding Catholic Women

Despite the fact that Catholic women have been barred from most powerful positions within the Church, they have not been without influence, as the following life stories will attest.

Queen Isabella (1451–1504). Known as *La Católica*, Isabella of Spain had a strong will and high moral standards from an early age. Since she stood to inherit a large chunk of Spain, the question of her future marriage became a federal case. Years of fending off many unsuitable suitors ended with her marriage to Ferdinand of Aragon, the prince of her choice and a Catholic to boot.

Isabella was an energetic reformer who set up her court as a center of influence. She was also something of an influence herself. With her blue eyes, fair hair, and magnificent dresses and jewels, she cut a striking figure. But at the same time she was intensely pious and orthodox in her beliefs. In fact, *La Católica* was so devout that she spent her leisure time learning Latin.

Isabella's pet project was supporting Christopher Columbus on his voyage to America. Although the story that she offered to pledge her jewels to help finance the expedition cannot be verified, Isabella is credited with making the decision to approve the momentous voyage. What a great opportunity to spread Christianity, thought Isabella, who was undoubtedly relieved that she could do so without becoming a missionary.

Lucrezia Borgia (1480–1519). Here's a lady as sinister as they come in the Catholic Church. As the daughter of a Spanish cardinal (who later became Pope Alexander VI) and his Roman mistress, Lucrezia's pedigree certainly reflects the tone of the Italian Renaissance. Not exactly what you'd call a good Catholic girl, she had a nasty reputation for treachery and lust. Because of her association with the evil deeds of her father and her brother Cesare, she made a name for herself as the feminine epitome of moral corruption.

Before she was twenty-two, she was twice promised in marriage to Spanish noblemen, but ended up marrying three Italian princes (not all at once) for reasons of political expediency. Her first marriage was annulled, and she was widowed when husband number two was wounded by some would-be assassins on the steps of St. Peter's and later strangled.

A few years later, a mysterious three-year-old child named Giovanni was seen with Lucrezia. There was much speculation about the identity of the child's father, but the smart money was on Lucrezia's brother or her father. This, plus her attendance at a celebrated orgy at the Vatican, bolstered the rumors of incest in the Borgia family. Lucrezia married another Italian nobleman, whose family wasn't thrilled that their son was marrying into a family with such an unsavory reputation. But Lucrezia cleaned up her act. After her pop the Pope died, she ceased to be a political tool of her family. She wisely turned to religion and died at the age of thirty-nine.

St. Joan of Arc (1412–31). It wasn't any desire to join the army that inspired the devout Joan to be all that she could be. By the time she was thirteen, Joan was hearing the voices of St. Michael, St. Catherine, and St. Margaret. These voices persuaded her that God had chosen her to help King Charles VII drive the English from French soil.

Charles was doubtful at first, but then believed Joan when she gave him a secret sign that to this day has never been revealed. With the king's okay, Joan set out with her army and rescued Orléans from the English in only ten days. She was wounded by an arrow in her breast, which made her even more of a hero.

Instead of resting on her laurels, Joan tried to reenact her victory, this time in Paris. She was cut off from the troops and captured by the English. Charles—the cad—made no attempt to save her. She was imprisoned at Rouen, tried for witchcraft and heresy, and burned at the stake.

Mary Tudor (1516–58). Queen Mary I was a devout Catholic who tried to draw England back to the One True Faith, which her father, Henry VIII, had ditched. This plan did not work out.

When her father divorced her mother to marry Anne Boleyn, Mary was told to enter a convent, but refused. Soon Anne was out of the picture (chop-chop). After her half brother, Edward VI, died, Mary was bumped up to queen. She married Philip II of Spain and restored Catholicism to England. So devoted was she to her faith that she burned almost three hundred heretics (read: Protestants) at the stake. Because of these persecutions, Mary picked up her colorful epithet: Bloody Mary. The cocktail came later.

Since she failed to produce a Catholic heir, Mary was succeeded by her Protestant half sister, Elizabeth I. There went the country.

†
EVEN MORE FAMOUS CATHOLICS

Pat Buchanan
Danny DeVito
Chris Evert
Walker Percy
Mary Gordon
John Gotti
Jon Bon Jovi
Spencer Tracy
Thomas Merton
Sinéad O'Connor
Jean-Bertrand Aristide
Jimmy Buffett
Terry Anderson
Anna Quindlen
Martin Scorsese
Ann Jillian
Alfonse D'Amato
Mickey Rourke
Mia Farrow
Clarence Thomas
Germaine Greer
Tony Bennett
Pat Conroy
Moises Alou
Kathleen Sullivan

Gabriela Sabatini
Tom Foley
Pierce Brosnan
Diane English
Lee Atwater
Jack O'Brien
William Wharton
Richard Daley, Jr.
Harry Connick, Jr.
Andy Garcia
Fay Vincent
Daniel Patrick Moynihan
Arnold Schwarzenegger
Mary Robinson
Roseanne Cash
Liam Neeson
Kimberly Bergalis
Lawrence Welk
Antonin Scalia
Bob Kerrey
Martin Sheen
Bono
Sonny Bono
Cher
Charo

AN ALMOST-CATHOLIC PRESIDENT:
William Jefferson Clinton

Sure, President Bill Clinton is a born and bred Southern Baptist, but several of his life experiences put him in the category of honorary Catholic. Witness:

- Attended Catholic school for two years as a child. His mother, Virginia Kelley, praised the effects of the nuns' discipline on a sometimes rambunctious little boy.
- Graduated from the Foreign Service School of Georgetown University, becoming the first U.S. president to graduate from a Catholic university.
- Considers JFK a personal hero.
- Mentioned the influence of Catholic social teaching on his political ideas in several major speeches.
- Received assistance in writing his Inaugural Address from Father Tim Healy, the late president of Georgetown.

RUBBING ELBOWS:
THE MOST CATHOLIC PLACES IN THE U.S.

The dioceses in the United States with the highest percentage of Catholics are:

Brownsville, Texas	80.8%
El Paso, Texas	65.0%
Lafayette, Louisiana	64.6%
Providence, Rhode Island	64.5%
Houma-Thibodaux, Louisiana	56.8%

GETTING AWAY FROM THEM ALL:

THE LEAST CATHOLIC PLACES IN THE U.S.

The dioceses in the United States with the lowest percentage of Catholics are:

Knoxville, Tennessee	1.8%
Savannah, Georgia	2.3%
Birmingham, Alabama	2.4%
Charlotte, North Carolina	2.5%
Tyler, Texas	2.8%

IT'S ALL IN THE FAMILY VALUES:
Great Catholic Dynasties

The Kennedys, of course, remain the premier American Catholic family. In the past, other Catholic dynasties—the Medicis, the Borgheses, the Borgias, and half the royal houses of Europe—left an indelible impression on history. All of these families are known as much for the drama of their personal lives as for their public achievements. There are a few who carry on in this grand tradition today.

The Grimaldis. Here's a clan whose escapades make page one of the *National Enquirer* almost as often as those of the British royal family. Princess Caroline, the fun-loving elder daughter, married a world-class playboy against the advice of the whole world. The Pope

himself annulled the marriage. Her second marriage ended in tragedy when her husband was killed in a speedboat race. Her younger sister, Princess Stephanie, has tried her hand at a number of glamorous careers—rock singer, model, swimsuit designer, and topless dancer. In love with her bodyguard, Stephanie raced to the altar a few weeks after the birth of their first child. The American-educated heir to the throne, Prince Albert, remains a bachelor.

The Graces. Dull by comparison with the Grimaldis (what family isn't?), the Graces have made their name in business and politics. The current patriarch of this family and the head of W. R. Grace & Company, Peter Grace, is one of the most

influential conservative lay Catholics in America. He is a close friend of Cardinal O'Connor and during the Reagan-Bush years was a supporter of the contras in Nicaragua, whose relations with the Church were sometimes rocky, to say the least. He once referred to New York Governor Mario Cuomo as "Cuomo the Homo" and New York City Mayor David Dinkins as "Dinkins the Pinkins."

The Hearsts. The Hearsts have provided entertainment for generations of Americans, and not just through their communications conglomerate. The antics of Patty/Tanya kept the nation in thrall for years, while the flamboyant life of her grandfather, William Randolph Hearst, was the basis for the classic film *Citizen Kane*. His newspapers, the foundation of the Hearst empire, were pretty sensational too: so rousing, in fact, that they started the Spanish-American War. Hearst's outrageously baroque estate in San Simeon, California—a town named, paradoxically, after an ascetic saint—is open to the public. The family currently owns a vast communications network that includes TV and radio stations, newspapers, magazines, and book publishers.

HOLLYWOOD'S HEAVENLY HITS:
Movies About Catholics

Filmmakers continue to offer up tales with Catholic themes, fascinated by priests, nuns, sin, and what they see as truly outrageous sexual practices, such as celibacy. Here are some of Hollywood's most notable recent efforts.

THE POPE MUST DIET. The name was changed from the original *The Pope Must Die* after a public outcry, despite the fact that most people would rather die than be called fat. The sequel will be changed from *The Pope Is Wasted* to *The Pope is Waisted.*

MOONSTRUCK. Cher plays an Italian-American widow who cheats on her fiancé with his brother and then goes to Confession to clear her conscience. Nowadays, it is more likely the priest would confess to Cher that he was having an affair with her fiancé's sister.

NUNS ON THE RUN. Two bumbling fools played by Eric Idle and Robbie Coltrane unwittingly get involved in mob activity and hide out from the bad guys by dressing up as nuns and taking refuge in a convent school, where they leer at scantily dressed coeds. Coltrane's *nom de veil* is Sister Euphemia of the Five Wounds—"Wounds" for short.

THE MISSION. Men of the cloth force their customs, rituals, and drab earth tones on a group of unsuspecting innocents. No, this is not a documentary on parochial school education, but the story of a Catholic missionary in the South American jungle.

SISTER ACT. Another entry in the "hardened ex-con hides out in convent and undergoes miraculous transformation" genre. The only miraculous thing here is that this may be the first movie in history to waste Maggie Smith's talent. Uses Motown score and features nuns singing "My Guy" as "My God." Thank God they didn't hit Broadway—we might have gotten "Everything's Coming Up Moses."

BORN ON THE FOURTH OF JULY. Crippled Vietnam War veteran played by Tom Cruise comes home embittered and emotionally scarred. He upsets his devoutly Catholic mother by yelling naughty words at her.

THE GODFATHER PART III. Michael Corleone, the worst guy in the world, lucks out by getting the kindest priest in the world the one time he goes to Confession.

MY LEFT FOOT. Should have been called *My Right Arm,* which is what Christy Brown's mother, a good Irish Catholic lady with twenty-three children, would have given for permission to use birth control.

Sinful Sequels We're Bound to See

Moviemakers have been offending the Catholic establishment for decades. Even though the official Church rating system has been abolished, most of the following films would merit a C—for "condemned"—if they were made today.

THE POPE OF GREENWICH VILLAGE II. The first openly gay pontiff, Lance I, moves the Vatican to New York's Christopher Street and declares that men can be nuns.

SINGLE WHITE FEMALE II. A futuristic tale in which the last surviving nun is discovered living in the abandoned convent of Our Lady of Perpetual Hope in Ho-Ho-Kus, New Jersey.

BOYZ N THE HOOD II. A follow-up to the smash hit *Sister Act,* in which three homeboys on the run from the Crips in South-Central L.A. hide out in a remote Franciscan monastery in the California desert. Starring Ice-T, with Sir Ian McKellen as the abbot.

MALCOLM XII. Spike Lee's magnificent five-and-a-half-hour epic biography of Malcolm XII, the first black Pope.

NOT THIS CENTURY, DEAR:
The Canonical Erection

With all the anxiety about sex in the Church these days, it is hardly surprising that mention is rarely made of a little-known ritual called a canonical erection. In fact, a canonical erection has nothing to do with sex, although the name certainly is a conversation stopper, isn't it?

A canonical erection is the rite by which the house of a religious order is sanctified and officially recognized by the Church. It was instituted as a regulating mechanism in the days when religious orders were springing up almost as quickly as Gap stores are today.

BESTCHESTER
COUNTRY CLUB
FORMERLY
OUR LADY OF SACRED
HEART CONVENT

Today, with the radical shrinking of most religious orders, we are much more likely to hear of a canonical suppression—the official closing and desanctifying of a religious house. There is a real element of sadness to these rites, as stately residences come to the end of their religious lives. But most religious orders these days need lots of cash to care for their retired members, not living space for hundreds. Happily, most religious houses sit on extremely valuable real estate—riverbanks, seashores, lakefronts, and hilltops.

Many former religious estates therefore undergo "conversion" into condos, resorts, golf courses, or schools. Others end up as headquarters for that uniquely modern quest for salvation—the drug and alcohol treatment program.

---

†
LOS CATÓLICOS HISPANOS:

DATOS Y ESTADÍSTICAS

- *Los Católicos hispanos actualmente forman la tercera parte de la población católica en los Estados Unidos.*
- *Los Católicos hispanos formarán la mitad de la población católica en los Estados Unidos en el año 2000.*
- *La iglesia católica pierde actualmente 60,000 católicos hispanos cada año a los predicadores protestantes fundamentalistas a los cuales el papa Juan Pablo II se ha referido como "lobos rapaces."*

HISPANIC CATHOLICS: FACTS AND FIGURES

- Hispanic Catholics now make up approximately one third of the U.S. Catholic population.
- Hispanics will make up half of the U.S. Catholic population by the year 2000.
- The Catholic Church is losing 60,000 Hispanic Catholics a year to Protestant fundamentalist preachers, whom Pope John Paul II has referred to as "rapacious wolves."

HOW WE'RE DOING:

CATHOLIC FACTS AND FIGURES

According to the *1993 Catholic Almanac:*

THE BAD NEWS

- There were 58,267,424 Catholics in the United States, 300,000 fewer than the previous year.
- The number of priests stood at 52,277, down 800.
- The number of nuns dropped below 100,000 for the first time in many decades. The new figure was 99,337, which reflects a loss of more than 2,500 in the past year and more than 22,000 in the past decade.
- Religious brothers numbered 6,603, dropping from 6,896.
- Only about 332,000 Catholic marriages were performed, down 4,000 from the previous year, and the lowest figure recorded since the early 1960s, when there were only about two-thirds as many U.S. Catholics as there are today.

THE GOOD NEWS

- The number of priestly ordinations increased to 864 from 620 the previous year.
- Permanent deacons rose in number to 10,384, which is 264 more than the year before and almost double the number of a decade ago.
- The number of baptisms or initiations of baptized Christians from other religions increased by nearly 33,000 to 1,180,707.
- Approximately 2 million U.S. Catholics are African-American, up almost 100 percent in four years.
- 453,000 Catholic deaths were reported, about 4,000 fewer than in the previous year.
- There were more parishes, students in Catholic elementary schools and colleges, Confirmations, First Communions, and Catholic health care and social service agencies.

V

EVERY-
THING'S UP
TO DATE IN
VATICAN CITY

CHRIST

Invisible Head of Church

Visible Head of Church

TIARA

POPE - Successor of St. Peter

MITRE

ALL BISHOPS
Successors of Apostles

BIRETTA

PRIESTS (Pastors)

REV. BROTHERS AND SISTERS

ALL OTHER CATHOLICS

Men
Women
Children

LAITY

SORRY ABOUT THAT!:
The Church and Science

Some people think that the Church moves slower than an IRS refund or an army discharge, but the fact is that all bureaucracies move at their own pace. Any complaints about the Church's sluggish tempo regarding Galileo Galilei, however, are certainly justifiable.

You might be aware that about 350 years ago, Galileo was brought before the Inquisition because of his heretical

findings on the nature of the universe. Galileo believed that the sun stood at the center of our solar system and that the earth moved around it. The Church, of course, maintained that the earth was the center of the universe. Galileo was forced to recant his findings, lest he find out how the burning gridiron feels. He took his medicine, but couldn't resist saying to the Church fathers, "Okay, but I'm still right." (Actually, what he said was *"Eppur si muove!"* which amounted to the same thing.)

Finally, after much study and careful deliberation, in 1992 the Church decided that Galileo was right after all, and opened an inquiry to determine how it could have been so close-minded. The Vatican also made plans to look into several other long-standing controversies in which Church doctrine and common sense seem to be at odds. The following cases are reportedly under consideration.

The *Horseless Carriage.* Since the advent of the automobile, the Church has feared that this invention might displace the horse from its God-given role as humankind's chief mode of transportation. Also, Pope Leo XIII was said to have had a horrifying vision of nuns driving.

The Moon Walk. Did men actually walk on the moon? The Church still officially believes that a Hollywood film set was used to deceive the population of the earth into thinking that astronauts traveled to the moon. The Church maintains that only angels can fly and that all scheduled airline flights are a hoax.

Babe Ruth's Called Home Run. Did the Babe actually point to the seats at Wrigley Field and call his own homer? Since Ruth was a Catholic, the Church is perfectly prepared to believe that divine intervention may have been the cause of this apparent miracle. Because news footage of the event is not definitive, however, the Church will reserve judgment until the next remake of *The Babe Ruth Story.*

NOTHING COMPARES 2 U:
Sinéad and the Pope

The single most notable event in the international Catholic year 1992 was not a proclamation from the Vatican or the most recent bishops' conference. No, it was when a bald Irish rock singer, performing live on American television, tore up a picture of Pope John Paul II. As the replays and freeze-frames of the ceremonial Pope-ripping flashed across the

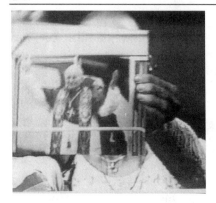 

airwaves and the news wires, Sinéad O'Connor loosed a firestorm of controversy not seen since John Lennon said he thought the Beatles were more popular than Jesus Christ.

If a picture is worth a thousand words, then ripping one up is worth a million. From *The New Republic* to the *National Enquirer*, the press suddenly had a topic to rival the latest Elvis sighting or bootlegged tapes of Charles' and Di's steamy telephone trysts. Sinéad got booed off stages and vilified by fellow rock stars. She was pilloried in the mainstream press for insulting millions of Catholics, even though many of these affronted millions hadn't been to Mass in years.

This wasn't the first time, of course, that Sinéad had caused a stir. There was her refusal to appear at the Grammy Awards show, and her famous prohibition against having "The Star-Spangled Banner" played before her concerts. But even Sinéad seemed unprepared for the response to her Pope-trashing. There were demonstrations in which her recordings were crushed by bulldozers—the audio version of book burning. "Sinéad Brigades" formed in her defense. Wearing Sinéad masks, they held counterdemonstrations in which they, too, tore up pictures of the Pope.

Yet in the midst of this maelstrom, has there been any word from the Offended Party himself? Where is the press release from the Vatican, the "How dare you?" from the halls of the Holy See? Regardless of how you feel about the singer, the show, or even the thought behind the symbolic act, remember that you haven't heard a peep about it from the Pope.

THINGS CATHOLICS SAID WHEN SINÉAD RIPPED THE POPE

"On TV?! Omigod!"
"I've got that same picture on a holy card."
"The s— is really going to hit the fan."
"She is so-o-o-o outspoken."
"Isn't she going out with Peter Gabriel?"
"Cool."
"I'm calling Mom right now."
"Did you see that?! Did you see that?!"

PAPAL POOP:
An Unofficial Who's Who of Popes

St. Peter the Apostle was the first, and 301 popes later (including antipopes), John Paul II became the latest in line. Who were these remarkable men? Here's a little background on some of our more colorful Church leaders.

Fabian (236–50). Great name. Pretty great Pope too, from the sketchy details known of his life. He is most remembered for the way in which he was selected to be Pope. According to Eusebius, a later Pope, a dove landed on Fabian's head as the clergy were mulling over names. Even though no one had considered Fabian a candidate, he got the job. Who's to argue with the Holy Spirit?

Martin I (649–53). Martin was known for his independent spirit, which got him into trouble when he had himself consecrated without getting the permission of the Holy Roman Emperor, who then refused to recognize him as Pope. Martin ignored the rebuff, so the emperor had him arrested, deposed, and shipped off to Constantinople to live out his last years in solitary confinement. He resigned himself to his fate and prayed until he died from cold, starvation, and harsh treatment. It was not long before the Church came to venerate him as a martyr.

Stephen (II) (752). Stephen (II), as he is commonly known, was elected and installed as Pope in 752. He had a stroke three days after the election and died the following day. He is perhaps best known for messing up the numberings of popes with the same name, who are usually referred to as Stephen II (III), Steven III (IV), Stephen IV (V), and so on.

Formosus (891–96). Formosus didn't have many enemies, but one of them was his successor, Stephen VI (VII), who had extremely bizarre ideas about turning the other cheek. Nine months after Formosus' death, Stephen had the body exhumed and propped up on a throne in full pontifical vestments. Stephen went on to preside over a mock trial, in which (surprise!) Formosus was found guilty of perjury, of having coveted the papal throne, and of a few other infractions. Stephen declared all his predecessor's acts and ordinations to be null and void, and tossed Formosus' body into the Tiber River. A hermit found it. Soon there were reports of miracles worked by the mutilated corpse. The following year, a friendlier Pope ordered Formosus to be reburied in his original grave in St. Peter's.

John XII (955–64). Just eighteen when elected, John kept Roman tongues wagging with his disinterest in the spiritual life and his fondness for boorish pleasures. Gossip that this bad-boy Pope was turning the papal palace into a brothel was given credence when he had a stroke, allegedly while in bed with a married woman. He died a week later, still only in his mid-twenties.

Celestine IV (1294–96). After two years without a Pope, feuding cardinals heard that a devout hermit had prophesied heavenly retribution if the Church went without a leader much longer. In the hope that a bold stroke would rejuvenate the papacy, they elected the hermit, who accepted under extreme duress. Celestine was eighty-five years old when elected, the eleventh child of Italian peasants. As a teenager, he entered a Benedictine monastery, but was drawn to the solitary life and lived by himself in a cave for many years. He seemed not to like being Pope, and wanted to hand over the papacy to a few cardinals so he could fast and pray. This offer was rejected. Stripping off his papal insignia and begging to be allowed to return to his cave, Celestine was detained under guard. He escaped for several months, but was captured and locked in a castle tower until his death.

John XXI (1276–77). Many Popes throughout history were writers, but John is probably the only Pope who wrote a published work on ophthalmol-

ogy, called *The Eye.* As irritating to papal list makers as Stephen (II), he bungled the numberings for Johns when—oops—he forgot that there was no XX and called himself XXI. John died an untimely death when the ceiling of his study collapsed on him.

Urban VI (1378–89). Urban was elected amidst a swirl of French-Roman competition for popehood. Crowds demonstrated in the streets of Rome, begging for a Roman, or at least an Italian, as the next Pope. In a panic-stricken session, the cardinals acquiesced and voted for Urban. No one knew about his stubbornness, violent recalcitrance, and general mental instability. After being pushed to their limits by the Pope's uncontrollable tirades, the cardinals met secretly. Urban rejected their "invitation" to abdi-

cate, and at that point, the cardinals informed the world that he had been deposed. They elected a new Pope, Clement VII, which brought about what is known as the Great Schism. Urban and Clement, after officially excommunicating one another, spent their days sending out letters all over Europe in which each claimed to be the true Pope. A war ensued, along with much plotting, intrigue, tortured cardinals, poisonings, and the like.

Leo X (1513–21). This spendthrift was a Renaissance man who loved nothing more than to patronize the arts. But he also had wars and crusades to pay for. On top of that, the construction of St. Peter's was costing a bundle. Unfortunately for the financially strapped Pope, parish bazaars had not yet been invented. He pawned the palace furniture, borrowed extensively, sold cardinalships and other offices, and renewed the selling of indulgences. Leo died suddenly of malaria, leaving the papal treasury deeply in debt.

John Paul I (1978). He remarked that he might have become a journalist if he had not become a priest. He wrote a collection of fanciful but incisive letters to authors and characters in history and fiction, including Pinocchio and Figaro. He chose his papal name in a desire to combine the progressive and traditional qualities of the two previous Popes. After his election, he held a spontaneous press conference, where he enraptured thousands of journalists. John Paul's reign was cut short by an untimely heart attack after he had been

in office only three weeks. Rumors of foul play followed, incited by a report that he was poisoned because of his plan to clean up the Vatican Bank, but these rumors were never substantiated.

HOLY HANDLES:
Popes and Their Names

Hate your name?

You could always march down to City Hall and officially change it . . . or you could get yourself elected Pope.

Every new Pope gets to take a new name, although it is unlikely that any Pope followed his particular career path solely for that reason. Popes generally limit themselves to old-fashioned names and seem to have a predilection for large Roman numerals.

Let's take a look at some well-known people who have changed their names. See if you can tell who went to City Hall and who was elected Pope.

Given Name	Adopted Name
Samuel Clemens	Mark Twain
Cardinal MastaiFerretti	Pius IX
Richard Starkey	Ringo Starr
Cardinal Pecci	Leo XIII
Cardinal Sarto	Pius X
Leslie R. King	Gerald Ford
Gordon Sumner	Sting
Cardinal Della Chiesa	Benedict XV
Marion Morrison	John Wayne
Roy Harold Scherer, Jr.	Rock Hudson
Cardinal Achille Ratti	Piux XI
Cardinal Pacelli	Piux XII
Israel Baline	Irving Berlin
Cardinal Roncalli	John XXIII
Archibald Leach	Cary Grant
Cardinal Montini	Paul VI
Cardinal Luciani	John Paul I
Allen Konigsberg	Woody Allen
Cardinal Wojtyla	John Paul II

♰
POPE DOPE

Sergius I (678–89) was an accomplished singer who introduced the singing of the Agnus Dei (Lamb of God) at Mass.

John VIII (872–82) was the first Pope to be assassinated. He was poisoned by members of his entourage and clubbed to death.

Callistus III (1455–58) is the Pope who reopened the case of Joan of Arc, who was burned at the stake in 1431 on charges of witchcraft and heresy. Twenty-five years after her sentence, Callistus declared her innocent and reversed the original judgment.

Gregory XIV (1590–91) banned all betting on papal elections.

Gregory XV (1621–23) was the first Jesuit-trained Pope. He canonized several hall-of-fame saints, such as Theresa of Avila, Ignatius Loyola, and Francis Xavier.

Clement XIV (1769–74) supported the arts, but disenchanted artists by ordering that nudes in paintings be covered up, including the ones on the ceiling of the Sistine Chapel.

Pius X (1903–14) offended American Catholics when he refused to receive ex-President Theodore Roosevelt, who had been lecturing at the Methodist Church in Rome.

Pius XII (1939–58) permitted Roman Catholics to engage in discussions with non-Romans on matters of faith.

IL PAPA, MY BROTHER

Paul I (757–67) was elected upon the death of his elder brother, Stephen II (III) (752–57).

When Benedict VIII (1012–24) died, his well-connected family decided that his younger brother should have a turn. Extravagant bribery ensured that John XIX (1024–31) was upgraded from layman to Pope in a single day.

IL PAPA, MY SON

Hormisdas (514–23) and Silverius (536–37) were father and son.

IL PAPA, MY PAPA

Felix III (483–92) was a widower with at least two children.

Clement IV (1265–68) was a widower with two daughters when he became a priest.

Innocent VIII (1484–92) fathered several illegitimate children before his ordination. As Pope, he provided for them by arranging for them to marry into princely houses.

RENDER UNTO CAESAR:

**RECTORIES: $50 EACH. RENT: $10
FOUR RECTORIES
EQUAL ONE CHURCH
RENT: $200**

PUBLIC WORKS

RENT:
SIX TIMES THE
AMOUNT SHOWN
ON DICE FOR ONE:
TEN TIMES THE
THE AMOUNT
SHOWN ON DICE
FOR TWO:

WESTM

ST.   ST.

MO
CO
WH   RE
YO   2
FO

N CITY

ORTGAGE
$500

**PUBLIC WORKS
TITLE DEEDS
AND
STAIRWAYS TO HEAVEN**
COLLECT $50 FOR EACH
STAIRWAY YOU OWN

MIRACLE AT GUADALUPE   COLOGNE   ST. PETERS

VIA DOLOROSA

INDULGENCE CARD

WESTMINSTER

IL DUOMO

© BARKER BROS.

GO   ST. PATRICKS   VATICAN CITY

GA

$$$ The Board Game of Vatican Banking $$$

Now You Too Can Play Vatican Banker!
Share the Intrigue and Adventure of the Banco Ambrosiano
Scandal in *Render unto Caesar!*

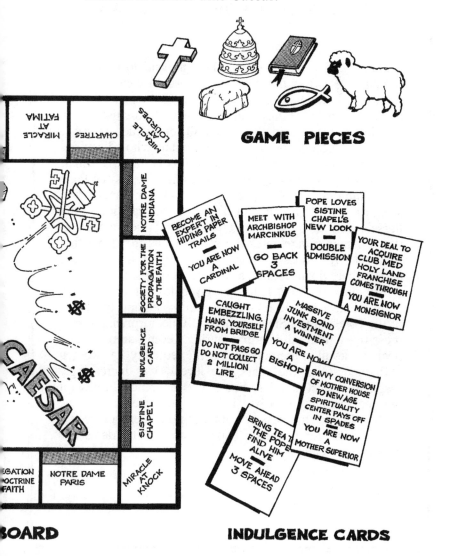

GAME PIECES

BOARD

INDULGENCE CARDS

WOMAN ON TOP:

THE LEGEND OF POPE JOAN

The legend of Pope Joan, who was said to have lived sometime between the ninth and eleventh centuries, became popular when her story appeared in print for the first time in the thirteenth century. A treatise by a Dominican priest said that when Victor III died in 1087, he was succeeded by a talented woman who, disguised as a man, had worked her way up to being a cardinal. The story goes on to report that one fine day, as the Pope was mounting her horse, she gave away her secret when she gave birth to a child. In disgrace, she was tied to the horse's tail, dragged around Rome, and then stoned to death. Another version of the story claims that from that time on, the Popes always took a detour to avoid the street where Joan became a Middle Ages mom.

The story of Pope Joan was given further credence in 1400 when a female figure was placed among the busts of the Popes in the Siena cathedral. One surprisingly progressive fourteenth-century writer even argued that Joan's elevation demonstrated the equality of women with men. Over the years, the legend was increasingly disparaged by Catholics, but it was a French Protestant who convincingly quashed it in the seventeenth century. A close look at the facts reveals that no contemporary evidence exists for a female Pope at any of the dates she supposedly reigned.

HIS PROMINENT EMINENCE:
Cardinal John J. O'Connor

Many Catholic bishops and cardinals take stands on controversial issues, but none gets more media attention than New York's Cardinal John J. O'Connor. True, O'Connor's bishopric (yes, it really is a word and it's not dirty) happens to contain the nation's media capital. But O'Connor himself seems to be one big walking sound bite. He sees himself as the Pope's leading spokesman in America, and St. Patrick's Cathedral gives him the country's most visible bully pulpit.

What follower of Catholic news can forget that he condemned satanic rock lyrics, reported that exorcisms are still being performed, and asserted that angels really *do* exist?

What about the time he criticized environmentalists for being more concerned with "whales and snails" than with people? Or the time he denounced "radical feminists" and insisted on the front page of the *New York Post* that "God Is a Man"?

By far the most famous O'Connor Occasion, however, was the "Siege of St. Pat's" a few years back, when AIDS activists demonstrated inside the cathedral during Mass. O'Connor told the press that anyone wanting to stop a Mass at St. Patrick's would do so "Over My Dead Body."

Always one to rush in where his beloved angels presumably fear to tread, O'Connor un-

doubtedly will continue to inspire, amuse, and infuriate before he reaches the mandatory retirement age of seventy-five.

CATHOLIC NEWS AROUND THE WORLD

NUNS MAKE PAX WITH FAX

LeBarroux, France—Cloistered nuns here recently got a fax machine, but transmit only in Latin.

EVERYTHING'S UP TO DATE IN VATICAN CITY

Rome, Italy—An Italian company is now selling customized confessionals with features the old guilt-box just didn't have. These include air-conditioning, presumably so that when the penitent (or the priest) gets a little hot under the collar about a particular sin or steamy revelation, the super-confessional can keep both parties cool and calm. Heating is also available. Since lots of churches apparently were built in the Stone Age, or at least built *of* stone, the old barns are not always warm enough for comfort. The new super-confessional blows a bit more hot air into the chamber than the penitent is already spewing. The customized confessional can also be sound-proofed. (Surprise! They never were!)

HOLE-Y VISIT FOR PONTIFF

Denver, Colorado—Before the Pope's planned trip to Denver in 1993, organizers were faced with an environmental dilemma unheard-of in the annals of papal globe-trotting. It seems that the site the organizers selected for the pontiff's hoedown is also home to a vast number of burrowing prairie dogs. These likable-looking creatures with a bark-like cry are a major part of the area's ecosystem, although a bane to humans who might step in the holes the little critters make. The organizers' answer to this problem: "hoover" the frisky suckers out with a vacuum, fill up the holes, and keep the varmints penned up for a few days until il Papa flies off into the sunset.

CHICAGO IS NO-GO FOR FOX

Berkeley, California—The controversial Dominican priest Matthew Fox continues to make news with his refusal to relocate from California to Chicago, even though he was asked to do so by the head of his order. Because of his unorthodox theological writings, Fox was officially silenced for one year by the Vatican.

Rev. Fox is head of the Institute for Culture and Creation Spirituality in Berkeley, which employs a masseuse, some Zen Buddhists, and a witch named Starhawk. Attempts to move Fox out of California prove once again that today's Church may be post–Vatican II, but for the most part it is not New Age.

PARTY ON!:
The Church Takes a Three-Day Weekend

For some time now, the U.S. government has been moving national holidays to Mondays so that Americans can enjoy a number of three-day weekends. Apparently following the government's lead, the Vatican has recently released new rules regarding Holy Days of Obligation. Starting in 1993, whenever the Feast of Mary (January 1) or the Feast of the Assumption (August 15) falls on a Monday or Saturday, Mass attendance is optional.

Lest American Catholics fear that the Church is making convenience its *sine qua non* (for those who don't know Latin, look it up), we remind them that they are still required to attend Mass on four other Holy Days of Obligation no matter what: Ascension Thursday in the sixth week after Easter; November 1, All Saints Day; December 8, the Feast of the Immaculate Conception; and December 25, Christmas.

GONNA TAKE A MIRACLE:
How Saints Are Made

The Christian Church has been venerating saints ever since the second century. For the early saints, there was no formal canonization process—they simply became saints by popular acclaim. And potential saints who pull in the crowds continue to be stronger possibilities for sainthood than holy nobodies. But for the past thousand years or so, saints have been formally chosen by the Sacred Congregation for the Causes of Saints, commonly known as "the saint factory."

Vatican II reforms pruned a Church calendar that was bursting with saints. But Pope John Paul II has more than made up for these recalls of early saints by becoming the biggest saintmaker in history. He has canonized 260 of the 700 official saints that have been recorded since the tenth century.

The Church is looking to broaden its cadre of saints, to seek out worthy Catholics who aren't part of the European white male contingent that makes up over half the saint roster. Since

most saints are priests, bishops, and nuns, an effort is being made to canonize more "regular folks" as well. Furthermore, potential saints are being searched out in lands just coming back into the fold of the faithful, such as the Eastern European countries. Perhaps not entirely by coincidence, there are great numbers of Poles on the docket, and these candidates are moving through the process with unusual alacrity. One potential saint whose controversial candidacy is progressing with extraordinary speed is that of Father Josemaría Escriva, the Spanish priest who founded Opus Dei, the ultraconservative Catholic organization.

The always-mysterious saint-making process has certainly come a long way over the years. In 1985 the saint-makers' office acquired its first two photocopy machines. Computers are now used, and documents no longer have to be handwritten in Latin. The prosecuting counsel, popularly known as the Devil's Advocate, has been eliminated from the proceedings.

Currently, there are more than 2,000 candidates for sainthood waiting for the nod. Their supporters bide their time as they try to meet the toughest requirement of all—proof of two miracles. Both miracles must occur after the candidate's death—one before beatification and one before canonization. But long before candidates get to that point, another miracle of a financial nature must take place, since the cost of promoting the average modern-day canonization is now in the neighborhood of $250,000.

PIERRE TOUSSAINT:
Is He or Isn't He? Only the Vatican Knows for Sure

With the tally standing at a paltry three, the United States has a pretty crummy record when it comes to saints. While Sisters Frances Cabrini and Elizabeth Seton, along with Bishop John Neumann, were fitting choices, isn't it time the lineup included more individuals that represent the diversity of America?

Maybe. The Vatican jury is still out on Pierre Toussaint, a candidate who just might become the first black saint of North America. An eighteenth-century Haitian slave, Toussaint worked on a plantation until a revolution forced his master's family, along with their servants, to flee to New York. When his master died, Toussaint became the extended family's breadwinner.

In a midlife career switch, he found himself hairdresser to a tony New York society crowd. But Toussaint didn't let life in the fast lane lead him astray. In his spare time, he worked to better the lives of the poor, raising funds to establish America's first Catholic orphanage as well as the country's first order of black nuns, the Sisters of Providence.

In 1989 New York's Cardinal John J. O'Connor initiated formal proceedings toward the canonization of Pierre Toussaint. As the Church looks to diversify its array of saints, Toussaint may be a strong contender. But while some applaud Toussaint's nomination, others charge that his subservient slave background makes him an inappropriate spiritual role model for today's black Catholics. He may or may not be a politically correct candidate, but only time will tell if he is Vatican Correct.

THE PATRONAGE GAME:
A 20th-Century Saints Matching Column

Remember that well-thumbed copy of *Lives of the Saints* from your childhood? And the thrill of reading about a saint whose life experience somehow connected with your own? Here's a chance to relive that experience, but with a contemporary twist. The following saints are indeed real, but their patronage has been updated.

Saint

1. St. Loman
2. St. Hermes
3. St. Conan
4. St. Basil
5. St. Thomas of Villanova
6. St. Arrowsmith

7. SS. Benedict and Florentius
8. St. Colman
9. St. Bean
10. St. Mylor
11. St. Vitalis
12. St. Fara
13. St. Cumin
14. St. Conran
15. St. Apollo

Patron of

A. Moon walkers
B. Overnight campers
C. Hairstylists
D. Taco stuffers
E. Girls with pouffed hair
F. Wearers of expensive French silk neckties
G. Trendy decorators
H. Pesto lovers
I. Pennsylvania basketball fans
J. Barbarians
K. Mail-order clothiers
L. Door-to-door sales reps
M. Brunch chefs
N. Buyers of silver balloon bouquets
O. Heavy metal rock bands

Answers:

1. L, 2. F, 3. J, 4. H, 5. I, 6. O, 7. M, 8. B, 9. K, 10. N, 11. C, 12. E, 13. D, 14. G, 15. A.

SAINT FUN FACTS

St. Patrick was born in Scotland.

The first person to see Jesus after he rose from the dead was **St. Mary Magdalene**, who mistook him for a gardener.

A legendary account of the life of **St. Barbara** says that she was shut up in a tower so no man would see her. She infuriated her father by becoming a Christian. This being Egypt in the second century A.D., a judge ordered her father to kill her but he was struck by lightning before he could do so. Barbara is the patron saint of those in sudden danger, especially those in danger of being struck by lightning, mines, or cannonballs.

St. Rose of Lima was originally christened Isabel, but her name was changed in infancy because of her likeness to the flower.

St. Lucy is often painted with her eyeballs in a dish, although there is no historical mention of her eyes having been plucked out during her martyrdom. Nonetheless, in some places her intercession is requested for diseases of the eye.

A legend surrounding **St. Nicholas**, Archbishop of Myra, tells that he is the patron saint of children, having brought back to life three children murdered in a brine tub. He gave them gifts and his name was later corrupted into Santa Claus. He is also known as the patron saint of unmarried women, having provided dowries for three women so that they would not have to become prostitutes.

Historical facts about her are rare and some scholars have doubted her existence, but word has it that **St. Brigid** was baptized by St. Patrick and became a nun at an early age. One miracle showed her compassion for others—she changed her bathwater into beer to satisfy the thirst of unexpected clerical visitors. St. Brigid is the patron of poets, blacksmiths, and healers. Her most unusual iconographical attribute is a cow lying at her feet, which some say recalls her phase as a nun-cowgirl.

Versatile twelfth-century nun **St. Hildegard of Bingen** was a mystic, a counselor to kings and Popes, a composer, a renowned preacher, and the founder of an abbey at Bingen, Germany. Big deal, you say. But she was also a homeopathic healer, and authored natural history studies on reptiles as well as medical works on giddiness and frenzy.

NOT A NICE PLACE TO VISIT:

Medjugorje, the New Lourdes

✝

The spectacular occurrences at the new shrine of Medjugorje are on everyone's lips these days—even though they can't pronounce it with their lips. For the record, it's pronounced *Med-u-GOR-yeh* and it is located in what is left of Yugoslavia. Since 1981, Mary has been seen there hundreds of times by children ranging in age from ten to eighteen. She has asked them to pray for world peace. (Obviously, they can't pray for godless communism to fall anymore.)

One of the many reported miracles of Medjugorje is that the sun spins wildly in the sky, and that you can look at it without damaging your eyes. (Caution: Do not try this at home.) Another reported miracle is that ordinary rosary beads turn to gold. Should you want to take a trip to this new holy place, check with the State Department first to determine whether the military situation is stable. You may be able to stare at the sun in safety, but no miracles have yet protected anyone from flying bullets or whizzing mortars.

The so-called miracles at Medjugorje meet many of the criteria used to determine authenticity, but not all.

Miracle Measure	Medjugorje
It happens in a remote village.	Yes
It happens to children.	Yes
Mary appears.	Yes
Whoever sees the miracle becomes a priest or a nun.	Too early to tell
A church is built on the site of the miracle.	On the drawing board
A movie is made about it.	Under development at major studio
It is sanctioned by the Church.	No

EPILOGUE:

STILL CATHOLIC

2001: A GRACE ODYSSEY:
The Catholic Church in the 21st Century

There is no doubt that the Church will change in the next decade just as it has done in the past. Here are a few of the changes that we might see in coming years.

1. Sinéad O'Connor will make a pilgrimage to Rome and personally apologize to the Pope for ripping up his picture on *Saturday Night Live* and calling him "the real enemy." She will correct herself by telling him that title is now reserved for Keanu Reeves, who refused to go out with her when she was last in the States.

2. Cardinal Bernardin of Chicago will be elected the first Pope of the American Catholic Church.

3. Madonna will fulfill her childhood dream of becoming a nun, and old-style black-and-white penguin habits will become the fashion rage.

4. Women will become priests, making much of local parish life "kinder and gentler."

5. The Vatican Bank will be declared insolvent and all Church holdings will be given to starving people all over the world . . . Oops! Sorry, that's the plot of *The Shoes of the Fisherman*.

6. Confessions will become such an important part of personal spiritual growth that they will be televised on a cable channel called SIN-TV.

7. The Russians will be converted to Christianity, fulfilling the promise of Our Lady of Fatima.

8. Tithing will be conducted by automatic bank transfer.

9. Drive-in Confession will be available at "Toot 'n' Tell" booths.

10. Anyone who was raised Catholic, converted to Catholicism, thought about being Catholic, or just doesn't get off on the "I'm an agnostic" rap anymore will think about where the real power of the Church on earth rests, which is in their hearts.

GOD REDUX

How are Catholics faring? What of those who went in search of new gods to replace the one they grew up with, or those who embraced the concept of a world where God had turned His back, was dead, or had never existed at all? Are they among the ones who read *The Road Less Traveled, Codependent No More, Healing the Shame That Binds You,* and *Life's Little Instruction Book?* What are these barely practicing or fallen-away Catholics searching for, and what will they find in today's Church if they have been away from it for a while?

Merely attending a once-a-week ceremony or maintaining a Catholic cultural tradition is evidently not enough for them. They seem to be looking for a greater sense of spirituality, both in their everyday lives and in their religious practice. They might be surprised to find, however, that in hundreds of parishes around the country other Catholics are trying to achieve exactly that. These Catholics are choosing service work—in soup kitchens, homeless shelters, AIDS hospices, and countless other places—rather than extra leisure time.

They are trying to bring about a transformation not only within other people's lives but within their own as well. These thoroughly contemporary Catholics are also looking again at many of the marvelous Church traditions that have been cast out over the past twenty-five years like so many babies with the Vatican II bathwater.

There will always be a human need to aim higher in life and to reach deeper within ourselves—to treat others with love and compassion, to develop more of our own potential, to make peace with the universe. So don't be surprised if someday on your way to an appointment, or after the kids have been dispatched to school, you find yourself sitting in the back pews of a church with just one or two others, looking far beyond the stained glass and remembering something you thought you had lost.

Mary Jane Frances Cavolina Meara was born in 1954 and grew up in the Bayside section of Queens, New York, where she attended Sacred Heart School. A model student, Jane once received a prayer book for never turning her head during Mass. She attended St. Mary's Girls' High School, where she perfected her understanding of the concept of purgatory, and went on to receive a B.A. Honors degree from Hunter College. Jane is currently a senior editor at Crown Publishers, and a coauthor, with her sister Ellen Cavolina, of *How to Really Watch The Godfather.* Still living (literally) in the shadow of her Catholic education, Jane resides next door to Sacred Heart School.

Jeffrey Allen Joseph Stone was born in Providence, Rhode Island, in 1955 and grew up in Westbrook and Gorham, Maine. He was baptized at an Italian parish in Providence, despite the fact that an associate pastor contended that neither "Jeffrey" nor "Allen" was a saint's name. Among his coauthors, Jeff is the only "public"—a public school student who attended CCD classes at a Catholic school on Saturdays and was accused, along with his fellow CCDers, of messing up the parochial kids' desks. Jeff graduated magna cum laude from Brown University in 1977. Now living in New York, he is a coauthor of *Treasures of the Aquarians* and *What Color Is Your Toothbrush?*

Maureen Anne Teresa Kelly was born in 1957 and was baptized at Most Precious Blood Church in Denver. Her first confession was said at St. Pius X Church in Dallas, and she received her First Holy Communion at Holy Ghost Church in Houston. In parochial school she won a glow-in-the-dark plastic Madonna for selling Holy Childhood Christmas Seals and was a member of the Junior Altar Rosary Society, an organization of young Catholic girls dedicated to straightening church pews and dusting kneelers. She went on to St. Agnes Academy in Houston and Randolph-Macon Woman's College in Lynchburg, Virginia. A coauthor of *Working in France,* she lives in Singapore.

Richard Glen Michael Davis was born in 1953 and was baptized at St. Valentine's Church in Cicero, Illinois. After attending Sacred Heart, St. Elizabeth of Hungary, Mary Queen of Heaven, and Christ the King schools, he graduated from Montini High School—Montini being the surname of Pope Paul VI—and went on to receive a B.A. from the University of Illinois. Richard, who lives in Chicago, is a author of *Treasures of the Aquarians* and *What Color Is Your Toothbrush?.*

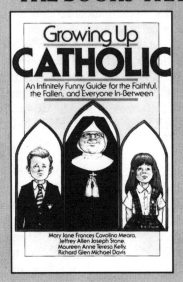
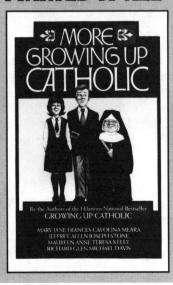